How to Do a
LIKE KIND EXCHANGE OF REAL ESTATE

Using a Qualified Intermediary

Or, how to **save thousands** of dollars in **taxes!!**

Edwin V. Horan, M.S., CES®

Certified Exchange Specialist®, Real Estate Broker
Senior Exchange Consultant, Realty Exchange Corporation
Member, Federation of Exchange Accommodators

North America & international
toll-free: 844-688-6899 (USA & Canada)
fax: 812 355 4082

About the Author

Ed Horan, CES®, is the founder and President Emeritus of Realty Exchange Corporation, a nationwide qualified intermediary. He currently serves as Treasurer and senior exchange consultant. Ed is a graduate of Syracuse University and George Washington University with a Master of Science degree in Business Administration.

Ed currently holds the Federation of Exchange Accommodators (FEA) prestigious professional designation of *"Certified Exchange Specialist®"*.

Ed has been frequent writer and lecturer on residential real estate investments, exchanges, and the impact of taxes on real estate transactions and real estate professionals. He is the editor of *Real Estate Exchange News*, a quarterly newsletter on current exchange topics. He is author of the real estate continuing education seminar text *"How-to-Do-a Like Kind Exchange — Using a Qualified Intermediary"*. He is the 1990 winner of the national Real Estate Educators Association award for the "Best Single Education Program".

Prior to 1981 Ed served as an officer, pilot and comptroller with the United States Air Force. Ed is currently licensed in Virginia as a real estate broker.

Dedication

This book is dedicated to my family. To my wife Jane, my two children Bill and Cindy, and four wonderful grandsons Kevin Joseph, Jeff, Max and Will. The support, love and understanding they continue to give me is greatly appreciated.

Acknowledgments

Any book on a subject as technical as Section 1031 of the Internal Revenue Code requires a great deal of research and study. I wish to acknowledge the authors of two books that I have used extensively over the years.

Jerry Long and Mary Foster are the authors of *Tax-Free Exchanges Under §1031,* the premier text and reference book for real estate, legal and accounting professionals involved in like kind exchanges. Their kind advice and assistance has been graciously given to me on many occasions.

Vernon Hoven is the author of *The Real Estate Investor's Tax Guide* which covers in depth the many tax topics that affect homeowners and real estate investors. The many examples and worksheets in his book make it a must own book for anyone involved in real estate sales, taxation and home ownership.

My children, Cynthia Dove and William Horan receive special acknowledgement for their devotion and hard work in taking over the reigns of Realty Exchange Corporation, our qualified intermediary company, so that I could devout more time to the writing and development of this book.

The staff and officers of the Federation of Exchange Accommodators (FEA) receive our special thanks for all of their efforts to keep the membership appraised of the many changes taking place with exchange legislation and IRS rulings. The establishment of the prestigious *Certified Exchange Specialist®* program has brought national recognition to those professional qualified intermediaries who have demonstrated their knowledge, experience and ethical behavior.

Contents

Appendix C

Index

Introduction

With the excellent appreciation of real estate over the years many owners of business, rental or investment real estate are faced with huge tax bills when they go to sell their appreciated real estate. Thus, this has led to an astonishing jump in the use nationwide of like kind exchanges. Thus, the need for this book.

A like kind or "Starker" exchange can provide for the deferral of these huge capital gain taxes. You may be advised by your real estate agent, tax advisor, CPA or a friendly neighbor of the wisdom of doing a like kind exchange. However, the details of how to actually do an exchange are usually lacking. In fact, more often then not you may receive bad information.

Internal Revenue Code Section 1031 and associated regulations provide the specific rules for successfully completing a like kind exchange of real estate. The regulations provide the "safe harbor" procedures that should be followed. If the "safe harbor" procedures are followed the IRS will not challenge the validity of the exchange. The "safe harbor" procedures require the use of a qualified intermediary to prepare and execute the documentation, effect the exchange and to safely hold the exchange escrow funds.

Since the IRS published the "final regulations" in 1991 the author has been giving seminars on how to do a like kind exchange and has been serving full time as a qualified intermediary. The seminar workbook used in the seminars has become a "must keep" reference tool. The updated and battle tested seminar workbook is the foundation for what follows in this book.

The author presents over 15 years experience as a qualified intermediary and instructor in telling you how to successfully complete a like kind exchange.

INTRODUCTION – HISTORY – CRITERIA – VACATION HOMES – RELATED PERSONS

1. EXCHANGE OF REAL ESTATE. It is a surprise to some that since 1921 investors have been able to exchange real estate. Only since the Tax Reform Act of 1986 made all capital gains fully taxable has the exchange of investment properties become more popular and essential if we are to avoid the taxes on capital gains. It is important that the small investor, real estate agent and other real estate professionals become fully aware of the advantages of an exchange, the IRS regulations covering an exchange, and how to actually execute the exchange. In this book we explain the critical elements of a tax deferred exchange and how they can be accomplished by the investor to meet accepted standards and IRS regulations.

2. HISTORY OF EXCHANGING. The basic law covering exchanging goes back to 1921. From that time until 1984 there was little change in the exchange rules.

In 1979, the rulings by the Ninth Circuit Court of Appeals in the famous Starker cases established the legal precedent that there could be a delay between transfer of ownership of the relinquished property and receipt of the replacement property.

As a direct result of the Starker decisions, Congress in the Tax Reform Act of 1984 amended IRC Section 1031, by adding subsection (a)(3), to establish the 45 day identification and 180 day settlement time limits for non simultaneous or delayed exchanges. This was a major legislative development that resolved the question of whether delayed exchanges were permitted under Section 1031. The 1984 Act also established that partnership interest could not be exchanged under Section 1031.

The Omnibus Budget Reconciliation Act of 1989 added §1031(f) that stated that exchanges between related parties would continue to qualify for deferral of gain provided neither the exchangor or the related person disposes within two years the property received in the exchange.

The 1989 Act also added subsection 1031(h) which provides that real property located in the United States and real property located outside the United Sates are not property of like kind.

The best news in the history of exchanging occurred when on May 1, 1991, the IRS published the final regulation which gives specific and clear guidance for the conduct of a tax deferred exchange. This regulation covers the role of the qualified intermediary, assignment of contracts, control of escrow funds, identification requirements, earning of interest and who is disqualified to act as a qualified intermediary or control the escrow account. This regulation greatly simplifies tax deferred exchanges and has revolutionized the exchange process.

In addition, in April 1990 an IRS Revenue Ruling authorized the use of a direct deed in an exchange, and IRS Form 8824 was published to simplify reporting of an exchange. The IRS Regulation was amended in April 1994 to coordinate the deferred like-kind exchange and installment sale rules.

The last major change to the exchange rules occurred in October 2000 when IRS Revenue Procedure 2000-37 was published to provide the rules to accommodate a reverse exchange. This "Safe Harbor" procedure provides for an Exchange Accommodation Titleholder (EAT). The EAT can purchase the relinquished property or the desired replacement property so that the taxpayer can proceed with the exchange (see Section 8).

Another change occurred in March 2002 when the IRS published Revenue Procedure 2002-22. This procedure states that commercial real estate sponsors who wish to sell "Tenancy-in-Common" (TIC) replacement property interests to exchangors can apply for a Private Letter Ruling (PLR) blessing the transaction. The procedure provides specific crite-ria that the sponsors should follow to obtain a favorable ruling (see page 7–4).

3. WHAT IS A TAX DEFERRED EXCHANGE? Section 1.1031(k)-1 of the regulation states:

> "A deferred exchange is defined as an exchange in which, pursuant to an **agreement**, the taxpayer **transfers property held** for productive use in a trade or business or for investment (the 'relinquished property') and **subsequently** receives property **to be held** either for productive use in a trade or business or for investment (the 'replacement property')."

4. CRITERIA FOR A TAX DEFERRED EXCHANGE OF LIKE KIND PROPERTY. To be a successful tax deferred exchange certain criteria must be met for the real estate to be **like-kind**. Basically these are:

1. Both properties must be in the United States.

For the Relinquished Property(ies)

2. The property currently must be used by the exchangor for investment, business or production of income.

   *It is **not** important how the buyer plans to use the property!!*

For the Replacement Property(ies)

3. The exchangor must hold the new property for investment, business and/or production of income.

   *It is **not** important how the property is currently being used by the seller!!*

4. The property must be identified in 45 days.

5. The property must be settled in 180 days (or the tax due date, including extension, if earlier).

It is not important that the purchaser buying the investor's property plans to use it as a personal residence; or that the property the exchangor acquires be currently used as a personal residence, an investment or business property. The property to be acquired can be currently used in any status—business, investment, dealer or personal. **The status of the currently owned property and the use the exchangor will make of the acquired replacement property is what is important!!**

5. WHAT IRC §1031 DOES NOT COVER. We know that Section 1031 provides for the exchange of a business or investment property for any other business or investment property. It is just as important to know what §1031 does not cover.

First, a **Principal Residence** cannot be included in an exchange under the provisions of §1031. Nor does a property to be immediately converted to a principal residence qualify as a like kind replacement property. See Appendix A, "Great Homeowners Tax Break" for a full explanation of the generous IRC Section 121 rules. Also see paragraph 10 in this Section.

Second, **dealer property** cannot be exchanged under IRC 1031 provisions. Dealer property is property held for resale, not for appreciation and/or income. A developer who purchases and resells lots could be considered a dealer. Also a contractor who buys and renovates homes and then immediately sells them could also be considered a dealer.

Third, **partnership interests** may not be exchanged under §1031. Many small investment or business properties are owned by partners. If title to the property is in the name of the partnership (example: "Smith Properties Partnership"), then the entire partnership must do the exchange. Individual partners may not exchange their interest because they have an interest in the partnership, and not in the real estate. However, if the property is deeded to individuals, as say "tenants-in-common", and they do not file a partnership tax return, then each partner may exchange their separate interest in the real estate, or pay the tax as they desire. Also, partners may use IRC Section 761(a) to elect out of the partnership and become eligible to exchange their interest in the property. Investors in a partnership should get tax and legal advice before engaging in an exchange.

6. SECOND HOME OR VACATION PROPERTY. Most tax practitioners agree that when a second home is used exclusively for personal use, it does not qualify for a Section 1031 Like Kind exchange. The difference in opinion occurs when the second home or vacation property is also rented out. There is no question that when the personal use of the vacation rental property is limited to 14 days or 10% of the days actually rented, whichever is greater, the property qualifies for a Like Kind exchange. Annual personal use of each rental property is reported on Schedule E of IRS Form 1040. (see Appendix A, page A-11 for copy of Schedule E).

If the personal use exceeds the 14 day or 10% of days actually rented rule, then the issue becomes whether the property is a non-qualifying second home or is still held for investment. IRS Section 280 establishes the rule to determine the amount of loss that can be deducted annually on a vacation rental property. If personal use is exceeded then loss deductions for the year are limited to gross rental income. If the personal use limit is not exceeded, then all the losses may be claimed.

Since there are no regulations, statutes or court cases which give a definitive answer in this situation, an exchangor should be able to support that the property was held for investment.

Owners of a vacation rental property need to coordinate with their tax adviser to determine if in their particular circumstances the property will qualify for a Like Kind exchange. Based on use a vacation property can change from investment property status to second home status from tax year to tax year. By planning ahead and restricting personal use in the year or two prior to the sale and after purchasing a replacement vacation property, there is no question the taxpayer will qualify for an exchange.

A day of personal use is defined in IRS Publication 527, *Residential Rental Property* (including Rental of Vacation Homes) and the Instructions for Schedule E as any day, or part of a day, that the unit was used by:

—the taxpayer for personal purposes
—any other person for personal purposes, if that person owns part of the unit, unless there is a shared equity financing agreement
— anyone in your family or that of a co-owner
—anyone who pays less than a fair rental price for the unit
—anyone under an agreement that lets the taxpayer use some other unit.

Not counted as personal use are any days spent working substantially full time repairing and maintaining the unit, even if family members use it for recreational purposes on that day.

7. REVERSE EXCHANGE. A true **reverse** exchange occurs when the replacement property is transferred to the exchangor before settlement of the relinquished property. A true reverse Starker exchange is still not permitted under §1031. In 2000 the IRS published Revenue Procedure 2000-37 which provides "safe harbor" procedures for the accommodation of reverse exchanges using an Exchange Accommodation Titleholder (EAT). See Section 8 for a complete explanation of the reverse exchange procedure.

Important — A replacement property may be placed under contract at any time — however, under §1031 you may not go to settlement on the replacement property until settlement on the relinquished property.

8. EXCHANGE WITH RELATED PERSON. An exchange may be made with a related party, however IRC Section 1031(f) imposes restrictions on such exchanges. Subsection (f) which was added to §1031 in 1989 denies non-recognition of the capital gain if either the related party or exchangor dispose of the property received within two years of the date of the last transfer which was part of the exchange.

Also, the IRS published Revenue Ruling 2002-83 on November 26, 2002, to address the applicability of IRC Section 1031(f)(4) to the purchase by an exchangor of the replacement property from a related party.

<u>If the exchange properties are held for two years it is clear that:</u>

First, an exchangor can do a related party direct exchange. A direct exchange occurs when the parties swap properties directly with each other. This normally occurs simultaneously and may involve a qualified intermediary.

Second, a related party can purchase the relinquished property. This is normally a deferred exchange using a Qualified Intermediary, with the exchangor buying the replacement property from an unrelated party.

However, regardless of the time the exchangor holds the new replacement property, or the use of a Qualified Intermediary, it is clear in the Revenue Ruling that purchase of the replacement property from a related party may result in the IRS disallowing the exchange. **Taxpayers should avoid the purchase of the replacement property from a related person**.

Exception. If the related party seller of the replacement property is not cashing out (that is, they are also doing an exchange), then the replacement property may be purchased from a related party. The requirement remains that the replacement property must be held for a period of two years.

A "related person" means any person bearing a relationship to the exchangor as set forth in IRC § 267(b) or 707(b)(1) and explained in IRS Publication 544. For example under these rules related parties include you and a member of your family (spouse, brother, sister, parent, child, etc.); you and a corporation in which you have more than 50% ownership; and you and a partnership/ LLC in which you own more than a 50% interest.

An in-law, aunt, uncle, cousin, nephew, niece or ex-spouse is not a related person. You should consult with your tax advisor if there is any doubt as to the related person status of the seller of the replacement property.

When an exchange is made with a related party then IRS Form 8824, which is used to report the exchange, must be filed for two additional years.

9. FOREIGN REAL PROPERTY EXCHANGES. Real property located in the United States and real property located outside of the United States are not considered like-kind property. Foreign real property is real property not located in a state or the District of Columbia. A foreign property may be exchanged for another foreign property. This restriction is imposed by IRC Section 1031(h).

Section **2**

Tax Impact Of A Sale Without An Exchange

1. SALE WITHOUT AN EXCHANGE. The first step to decide if we should simply sell and pay the tax, or exchange an investment property — is to estimate the tax due and the net sale proceeds after tax. For this we use the <u>Like Kind Exchange Analysis Worksheet</u> on page 2–5.

First, let us use the worksheet example to determine the potential Tax Due:

A. TAXABLE GAIN if property is sold

Selling Price		$500,000
Less: Estimated Selling Costs		−40,000
Adjusted Selling Price		$460,000
Original Cost Basis	$150,000	
Plus: Improvements	0	
Adjusted Cost Basis	= 150,000	
Less: All Depreciation Taken	−45,000	
Tax Basis		−105,000
Total Taxable Gain if property is sold		$355,000

B. FEDERAL TAX ON GAIN

Recapture of Section 1250 depreciation	
$45,000 X 25%	11,250
Capital Gain on Profit (Adj. Selling Price − Adj. Cost Basis)	
$310,000 X 15% *	+46,500
Total Federal Tax if Property is Sold	**$57,750**

   * For property transferred on or after May 6, 2003. Prior rate was 20%

2. SELLING COSTS. Our experience with the sale of small residential investment properties is that with commissions, points, attorney fees, etc. that 8% to 10% of the Selling Price is a good planning figure for Selling Costs. If a net sheet has been prepared by a real estate agent it will of course give a much better estimate of selling costs.

3. TAX BASIS. The owner's original Basis in the property is basically the purchase price with some additional acquisition costs. If the property was received in some other way, such as part of an exchange, an inheritance, on death of a spouse, or in a partnership distribution, you need to know what basis was assigned to the property when received. Any improvements to the property are added to the original basis. From that basis is subtracted all the depreciation that has been taken or was allowed over the years of ownership. In the above example, we assume that the property was purchased for $150,000, there were no improvements, and that all the depreciation taken while rented totals $45,000.

    We then subtract the Depreciation taken ($45,000) from the Basis ($150,000) and we have the Tax Basis of $105,000.

BASIS	$150,000
LESS: DEPRECIATION TAKEN	−45,000
TAX BASIS	$105,000

4. TOTAL TAXABLE GAIN. The taxable gain is the Adjusted Cost Basis subtracted from the Adjusted Selling Price.

ADJUSTED SELLING PRICE	$460,000
LESS: TAX BASIS	-105,000
TAXABLE GAIN	$355,000

REMEMBER – Taxable Gain is the Profit plus all the Depreciation taken.

ADJUSTED SELLING PRICE	$460,000
LESS: ADJ. COST BASIS	−150,000
PROFIT	$310,000
PLUS: DEPRECIATION	+45,000
TAXABLE GAIN	$355,000

If the property is Sold this is the amount that will be added to Taxable Income – this is the amount of Capital Gain !!

5. TAX DUE. While lowering the long term capital gains rate the Taxpayer Relief Act of 1997 (TRA 97) complicated the computation of the tax due on the sale or exchange of rental property by creating a separate 25% tax rate for depreciation recapture of Section 1250 property. The Jobs and Growth Tax Relief Reconciliation Act of 2003 lowered the capital gains rate from 20% to 15% for property transferred on or after May 6, 2003.

Part B, Line 10.a. on the worksheet provides for the recapture of depreciation on Section 1250 property. Section 1250 property is basically real estate rental property. If the property is sold all the depreciation taken (not in excess of total gain) is taxed at 25%.

Line 10.b. provides for the capital gains tax on the profit or remaining gain. The federal long term capital gain rate is **15%** or 5% for those in the 10 or 15% tax bracket.

If the property is sold the Federal TAX DUE will be $57,750

Recapture of Depreciation	$11,250
($45,000 at 25%)	
plus: Capital Gain on Profit	
($310,000 at 15%)	46,500
TAX DUE	$57,500

   Note: Additional State tax may also be due if the property is sold.

6. NET SALE PROCEEDS. Part C. BEFORE and AFTER TAX PROCEEDS of the worksheet provides for the necessary computations to determine both the Sale Proceeds Before Tax and the Net Sale Proceeds After Tax. In our example we can see that $370,000 would be available before tax or $312,250 after the federal tax is paid.

7. EXCHANGE REINVESTMENT REQUIREMENTS. Part D. of the Worksheet provides the two critical dollar reinvestment requirements for deferral of all the gain and thus a tax free exchange.

For deferral of all the gain the replacement property(ies) must cost at least the Adjusted Selling Price (line 3 on the Worksheet) and the amount of cash reinvested must at least the proceeds before tax (line 16 on the Worksheet).

ADJUSTED SELLING PRICE	$460,000
PROCEEDS BEFORE TAX	370,000

8. BUY DOWN or CASH BOOT. If the new replacement properties cost less then the Adjusted Selling Price (line 3) OR the cash reinvested is less then the Proceeds Before Tax (line 16) then Capital Gain will be recognized and taxed on whichever amount of difference is greater. The recaptured Section 1250 depreciation will be taxed first.

9. CONVERSION OF PROPERTY. While it must be the intent of the exchangor to initially hold the replacement property for investment, business or rental purposes, circumstances can change which could cause the exchangor to convert the replacement property to their personal use. Most tax advisors suggest a residential replacement property be rented for at least one year before conversion to a principal residence or second home.

Thus, it is possible to combine a like kind exchange and a principal residence exclusion for significant tax savings. If the replacement property is converted to a principle residence after being held as a rental property, and the property is used as a principal residence for two years, then the taxpayer may exclude up to $250,000 ($500,000 if married filing jointly) of capital gain if the property is sold. In October 2004, H.R. 4520 was passed which revised IRC Section 121 to require a principal residence replacement property received as part of a like kind exchange to be owned for five years before it can qualify for the IRC 121 primary residence exclusion.

Only the depreciation taken after May 6, 1997, during the period when the now principal residence was a rental, must be recaptured. See Appendix A for "The Great Real Estate Tax Break".

To automatically complete the Like Kind Exchange Analysis go to www.1031.us and select *Capital Gain Calculator*.

LIKE KIND EXCHANGE ANALYSIS

The purpose of this form is to determine the tax impact if a property is sold and not exchanged, and to determine the reinvestment requirements for a tax free exchange.

A. TAXABLE GAIN if property is sold

1. SELLING PRICE		$500,000
2. Less: Selling Costs	– 40,000	
3. ADJUSTED SELLING PRICE		460,000
4. Original Cost Basis	$150,000	
5. Plus: Improvements	+ 0	
6. ADJUSTED COST BASIS	=150,000	
7. less: All depreciation allowed/ taken	–45,000	
8. TAX BASIS (subtract from line 3)		–105,000
9. TOTAL TAXABLE GAIN or (LOSS) if property is sold		$355,000

B. FEDERAL TAX ON GAIN

10. a. Recapture of Section 1250 depreciation

                      $45,000 X 25% $11,250

    b. Capital Gain on Profit (Adj. Selling Price – Adj. Cost Basis)

                      $310,000 X 15%   +46,500

11. Total Federal Tax if Property is Sold $57,750

or amount deferred if property is exchanged

C. BEFORE and AFTER TAX PROCEEDS

12. SELLING PRICE (line 1)	$500,000
13. Less: Balance Due on all Loans	– 90,000
14. EQUITY	=410,000
15. Less: Selling Costs (line 2)	– 40,000
16. Proceeds Before Tax (cash to Escrow in an Exchange)	$370,000
17. Less: Total Tax Due (line 11)	– 57,750
18. Net Sale Proceeds After Tax if property is Sold	$312,250

D. EXCHANGE REINVESTMENT REQUIREMENTS

For deferral of all gain the replacement property(ies) must cost at least $460,000 (line 3) and the amount of cash reinvested must be at least $370,000 (line 16). The balance of funds needed to purchase the new property(ies) may be borrowed and/ or be **new cash**.

If the new property(ies) cost less then line 3 **OR** the cash reinvested is less then line 16, then capital gain will be recognized and be taxed on whichever amount of difference is greater. The recaptured Section 1250 depreciation is taxed first.

LIKE KIND EXCHANGE ANALYSIS

The purpose of this form is to determine the tax impact if a property is sold and not exchanged, and to determine the reinvestment requirements for a tax free exchange. *See reverse for example and explanation.*

A. TAXABLE GAIN if property is sold

1. SELLING PRICE $_____
2. Less: Selling Costs   − _____
3. Equals ADJUSTED SELLING PRICE   =$_____
4. Original Cost Basis $_____
5. Plus: Improvements   + _____
6. Equals ADJUSTED COST BASIS   = _____
7. Less: All depreciation authorized/ taken − _____
8. Equals TAX BASIS (subtract from line 3)   − _____
9. TOTAL TAXABLE GAIN if property is sold or deferred if property is exchanged $_____

B. FEDERAL TAX ON GAIN

10. a. Recapture of all Section 1250 depreciation allowed
    $_____(line 7) X 25% $_____
    b. Capital Gain on Profit (Adj. Selling Price less Adj. Cost Basis)
    $_____(line 3 less line 6) X 15%   + _____
11. Total Federal Tax due if Property is Sold or amount deferred if property is exchanged $_____

C. BEFORE and AFTER TAX PROCEEDS

12. SELLING PRICE (line 1) $_____
13. Less: Balance Due on all Loans   − _____
14. EQUITY   = _____
15. Less: Selling Costs (line 2)   − _____
16. Proceeds Before Tax (cash to Escrow in an Exchange) $_____
17. Less: Total Federal Tax Due (line 11)   − _____
18. Net Sale Proceeds After Tax if property is Sold $_____

D. EXCHANGE REINVESTMENT REQUIREMENTS

For deferral of all gain the replacement property(ies) must cost at least $_____(line 3) and the amount of cash reinvested must be at least $_____ (line 16). The balance of funds needed to purchase the new property(ies) may be borrowed and/ or be **new** cash.

If the new property(ies) cost less then line 3 or the cash reinvested is less then line 16, then the capital gain will be recognized and be taxed on whichever amount of difference is greater. The recaptured Section 1250 depreciation will be taxed first.

Example & Explanation of Like Kind Exchange Analysis

The Like Kind Exchange Analysis is used to determine the tax impact if a property is sold and not exchanged, and to determine the reinvestment requirements for a tax free exchange.

Example: A rental property has a <u>selling price</u> of $500,000 and it is estimated the total <u>selling costs</u> will be $40,000. The property <u>costs</u> $150,000 when purchased ten years ago. No depreciable improvements have been made. The estimated <u>depreciation</u> taken is $45,000.

A. TAXABLE GAIN if property is sold
1. SELLING PRICE		$500,000
2. Less: Selling Costs (see Note 1)		– 40,000
3. equals ADJUSTED SELLING PRICE		$460,000
4. Original Cost Basis	$150,000	
5. Plus: Improvements	+ zero	
6. equals ADJUSTED COST BASIS	150,000	
7. Less: All depreciation authorized/ taken (see Note 2)	– 45,000	
8. equals TAX BASIS (subtract from line 3)		–105,000
9. TOTAL TAXABLE GAIN if property is sold		$355,000

B. FEDERAL TAX ON GAIN (see Note 3)
10. a. Recapture of all Section 1250 depreciation allowed (see Note 4)	
$45,000 X 25%	$11,250
b. Capital Gain on Profit (Adj. Selling Price less Adj. Cost Basis)	
$310,000 X 15%	+ 46,500
11. Total Federal Tax if Property is Sold	$57,750

C. BEFORE and AFTER TAX PROCEEDS
12. SELLING PRICE (line 1)	$500,000
13. Less: Balance Due on all Loans	– 90,000
14. EQUITY	= 410,000
15. Less: Selling Costs (line 2)	– 40,000
16. Proceeds Before Tax (cash to Escrow in an Exchange)	$370,000
17. Less: Total Federal Tax Due (line 11)	– 57,750
18. Net Sale Proceeds After Tax if property is Sold	$312,250

D. EXCHANGE REINVESTMENT REQUIREMENTS
For deferral of all gain the replacement property(ies) must cost at least $460,000 (line 3) and the amount of cash reinvested must be at least $370,000 (line 16). The balance of funds needed to purchase the new property(ies) may be borrowed and/or be new cash.

Notes: (1) To estimate selling costs use 8 to 10% considering points paid or allowances given by seller. (2) To estimate residential depreciation taken multiply purchase price of property being sold by 3%, times the number of years the property has been rented. (3) Total taxable gain is the Profit plus all the Depreciation taken. (4) Section 1250 property is basically all real estate rental property.

Notes

REINVESTMENT REQUIREMENTS

1. TOTAL DEFERRAL OF CAPITAL GAINS TAX. One of the primary objectives of a tax deferred exchange is to defer paying any tax on the gain realized—the potential capital gain. For an exchange to be totally tax free the reinvestment in the replacement property or properties must meet all the following rules:

Rules for Totally Tax Free Exchange

Rule 1

Replacement property(ies) must have an equal or greater acquisition cost then the adjusted selling price of the relinquished property(ies).

Rule 2

All the cash received from the transfer of the relinquished property must be reinvested.

Rule 3

Replacement property should have a new or assumed mortgage total that is equal to or greater then the debt paid off on the relinquished property — **or add new cash to offset the difference.**

Rule 4

Exchangor should not receive non-like property – including owner held notes, cash or personal property.

---

2. PROJECTED PURCHASE OF REPLACEMENT PROPERTY. In the previous section we determined using the Like Kind Exchange Analysis worksheet the projected adjusted selling price, mortgage totals and before tax cash proceeds for the proposed relinquished property. These were:

Adjusted Sales Price	$460,000
Sale Proceeds (Before Tax)	370,000
Balance Due on Loans	90,000

3. REINVESTMENT REQUIREMENTS. To be **totally tax free and defer all of the realized gain** — the potential capital gain — we must follow all of the above rules. Using our example we can see that the replacement property or properties purchased would have to have:

(1) an acquisition cost of at least $460,000,
(2) all of the $370,000 cash received reinvested, and
(3) new or assumed mortgages of at least $90,000 — or the exchangor must add or substitute new cash to reach that total.

4. ACQUISITION COST. The acquisition cost is the contract price plus the acquisition expenses which are part of the cost to acquire the property. Normally these are shown on the Settlement Statement. The acquisition expenses do not include prepaid items, such as real estate taxes and hazard insurance, or expenses associated with obtaining financing, such as points. The cash in the qualified escrow account may be used toward both the down payment and acquisition expenses. See page 9-9 in Section 9 for table of Exchange Expenses.

5. PARTIAL TAX DEFERRED EXCHANGE. It is possible that the situation will arise when the Exchangor wants or ends up receiving **BOOT** — that is taxable income. There are three basic sources of boot. These are —

a. **Cash Boot**. Cash proceeds received at settlement or at the end of the exchange process are taxable income up to the amount of the total realized gain. Using our example — the investor needs $50,000 in cash immediately and receives it at settlement of the relinquished property:

Sales Proceeds (Before Tax)	$370,000
Cash Received (Taxable Income)	50,000
Cash Reinvested	320,000

b. **Mortgage Boot**. Mortgage relief (the mortgages on the replacement properties are less then the total mortgages on the relinquished properties) also becomes BOOT and taxable income. **IMPORTANT**. However, new cash in — that is adding new cash to the down payment can offset mortgage relief. Again, using our example, let us say for some reason the total new mortgage debt on the replacement properties is only $50,000

Total Current Mortgages	$90,000
Total New Mortgages	50,000
Mortgage Boot (Taxable)	$40,000

Remember!! New cash can offset Mortgage Boot

c. **Non-Like Property Boot**. If the exchangor were to receive non-like property in the transaction, say an automobile, it is considered as taxable income at market value.

More common is when the exchangor takes back financing on the relinquished property. The value of the note received is considered Boot and is taxable gain. With proper planning the Note will be treated as an installment sale and will be taxed as the gain is received over the term of the loan. The fact that the Note is sold at settlement by the exchangor does not change this situation. If at all possible the exchangor should avoid taking back financing on the relinquished property. See Section 7 for handling of an Installment Sale and alternate treatment of a Note from the buyer

6. BOOT AND THE REDUCED PRICE FOR THE REPLACEMENT PROPERTY. If the exchangor decides to 'buy down' — that is to purchase a replacement property that has an acquisition cost less then the adjusted sale price of the relinquished property we know immediately that the exchangor will have some taxable income. If the exchangor purchased a replacement property that cost $410,000 we know there will be $50,000 of potential capital gain recognized. The purchaser can take all or part of the $50,000 in cash or can reduce the new mortgage amount.

For planning purposes, if you know in advance that the exchangor desires cash out from the transaction then you can reduce the target price for the replacement property.

For example: using our previous numbers, the exchangor wants $50,000 in cash at settlement of the relinquished property.

To be totally tax free acquisition cost should be at least:	$460,000
Exchangor desires cash out of	– 50,000
For balance of capital gain of $305,000 to be deferred	
the replacement property should cost at least:	$410,000

7. TAX ON BOOT. How will the $50,000 of boot be taxed? Unfortunately any gain recognized in an exchange will be first taxed at the 25% federal rate until all the Section 1250 depreciation taken has been recaptured. In our example, the total depreciation of $45,000 would be taxed at 25% and the remaining recognized gain of $5,000 would be taxed at 15%.

Caution: To avoid taxable boot, rent and security deposit adjustments should be made outside of closing.

8. SIZE OF LOAN. To avoid cash boot Exchangors should be careful that the **size of the loan** on the replacement property isn't so high that they inadvertently receive **taxable cash boot** back at settlement. However, exchangors may receive the **cash deposit they made** back from the settlement agent. To defer all of the tax — the cash received from the transfer of the relinquished property must be used as **down payment** on the replacement property. The **loan amount** will then be the difference between the amount needed to purchase the property and the down payment. Be certain that the amount of your loan on the replacement property does not result in your getting cash at settlement in excess of your personal earnest money deposit.

**Boot Offsetting Rule: Mortgage boot can be offset with new cash —
but cash boot cannot be offset with additional mortgage.**

9. SUSPENDED PASSIVE ACTIVITY LOSSES. Many rental property owners with high incomes have suspended passive losses. These occur when the net income from a taxpayer's rental property is a loss and they do not qualify for all or part of the $25,000 special allowance for rental real estate. If a taxpayer has suspended passive losses, they are shown on IRS Form 8582, Passive Activity Loss Limitations, in their federal tax return.

When planning to do an exchange it is important that rental property owners with suspended passive losses determine (1) the total dollar amount of current suspended losses, along with the amount projected for the current year (See column (b) of Worksheet #5, Form 8582, in the latest tax return for the current amount of suspended passive losses) and (2) the amount of <u>capital gain to be realized</u> if the property is sold.

The taxpayer should then consider the following options:

Option #1. If the property is sold outright (i.e. all the gain is recognized), then all of the suspended losses for that activity can be used to offset the recognized capital gain from the sale of the property.

Option #2. If boot will be recognized in the exchange, then the suspended loss for the specific property being exchanged can be used to offset the gain. For example, if there are $20,000 in suspended losses for the specific property being exchanged, then the taxpayer could take $20,000 in cash out (cash boot), and this amount will be offset by the $20,000 in suspended passive losses.

Option #3. If the property is not sold outright, or boot recognized, then any suspended passive losses not used will be carried forward to the replacement property.

**If a taxpayer has suspended passive losses and is contemplating
selling or exchanging their rental property it is important that they
discuss the best option with their tax advisor.**

For a complete explanation of passive activity see IRS Publication 925, Passive Activity and At-Risk Rules.

10. EXCEPTION FOR REAL ESTATE PROFESSIONALS. Generally, rental activities are passive activities even if a taxpayer materially participates in them. However, if you qualify as a real estate professional, rental real estate activities in which you materially participate are not passive activities. You qualify as a real estate professional for the year if you meet both of the following requirements: first, one half of all business services performed were in real property businesses in which you materially participated, and second, you performed more than 750 hours in real property businesses. See page 5, IRS Publication 925, for a full explanation of this very favorable rule.

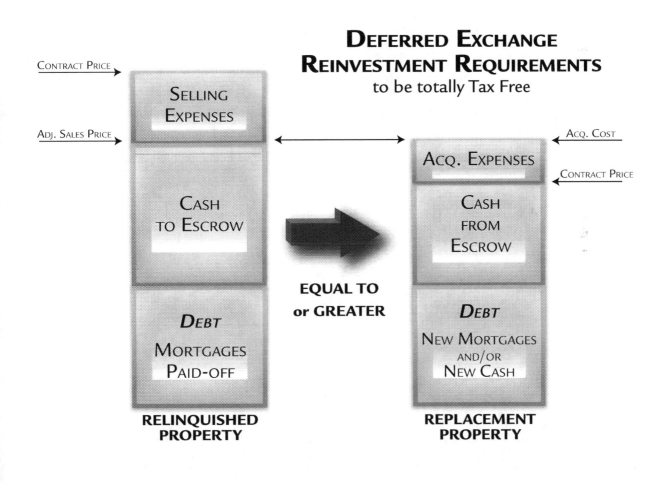

Notes

4

Critical Elements Of An Exchange

1. FIVE CRITICAL ELEMENTS. Because the IRS is more likely to review a tax free exchange transaction then the normal taxable sale it is important that the Exchangor comply with the strict requirements for an Exchange. The IRS requirements for control of the funds and the time limits for identification and receipt of the replacement property pertain primarily to deferred exchanges, and are the primary emphasis in the Section 1031 regulations published in 1991. The five critical elements are as follows:

a. **INTENT**. It should be the intent of the Investor from the start to the end of the transaction that the disposal of one property and the acquisition of another is meant to be an exchange.

b. **FORM and DOCUMENTATION**. To properly reflect the transaction as an exchange and not a sale – close compliance with the documentation requirements of the regulations is important. In Section 6 we review each document that is essential to the exchange process. Also provided in the Appendix is a checklist to assist exchangors meet all the exchange requirements.

c. **CONTROL OF FUNDS**. At no time in the delayed exchange process can the Exchangor have any control or otherwise obtain any benefits from the cash held in the exchange escrow account.

d. **LIKE-KIND PROPERTIES**. The properties exchanged must be investment or business properties that meet the "like kind" criteria. (See Section 1)

e. **TIME LIMITS**. The replacement exchange property must be identified within 45 days of settlement of the relinquished property and settled within 180 days. (See Section 5)

2. INTENT. From the start the intent of the owner of an investment property is very important. After a review of the taxes that will be due if the property is sold without an exchange — the owner may wish to dispose of the property as an exchange. If this is the case then it is desirable to begin from the start listing the property as an exchange. If later the owner decides not to do an exchange there is no harm done. However, if the listing starts out as a pure sale then a cloud occurs over the transaction if the decision is later made to do an exchange. So to show the early intent the following phrases <u>may</u> be added to the standard real estate broker listing agreement.

"It is the intent of the owner(s) to dispose of this property as a like kind exchange in accordance with IRC. Section 1031, and the owner requires the buyer to cooperate in the exchange."

It is also suggested that an Addendum showing the exchangors intent be added to the purchase contract for the relinquished property. See paragraph 4 in Section 6 and a sample Addendum on page A-7 of the Appendix. While a comment in the listing agreement and an Addendum to the contract are suggested they are not mandatory to complete the exchange.

3. CONTROL OF FUNDS. In a deferred exchange, gain or loss may be recognized (become taxable income) if the exchangors actually or constructively receive money or other property before they actually receive the like-kind replacement property. The exchangors are considered in actual receipt if they receive money or the economic benefit of the money or other property. They are in constructive receipt when the money is credited to their account or otherwise made available to them. The exchangor is not considered in receipt if substantial limitations or restrictions on receipt of the money or benefits exits. However, constructive receipt occurs when the limitations or restrictions lapse, expire or are waived.

To put it in the simplest terms:

The Exchangor can have no control of the exchange escrow funds!!

4. SAFE HARBORS. To avoid actual or constructive receipt exchangors may use the procedures or "safe harbors" established by the IRS in the 1991 regulations.

These are:

a. The use of a qualified escrow or trust account. A qualified escrow account exist when the account holder is not the exchangor or **a disqualified person**, and

**"the escrow agreement expressly limits the taxpayer's rights
to receive, pledge, borrow or otherwise obtain the benefits
of the cash or cash equivalent held in the escrow account".**

There are additional restrictions placed on disbursements from the exchange escrow account. These are know as the (g)(6) restrictions. In the event the exchangor does not identify replacement properties and wishes to terminate the exchange the holder of the escrow may not disburse any funds until the end of the 45 day identification period. Also if the exchangor properly identifies replacement properties then the escrow holder can only disburse funds if (a) the 180 day exchange period has passed, or (b) the exchangors have received all of the replacement property to which they are entitled under the agreement.

> **Warning:** There must be a specific written agreement between the exchangor and the party holding the escrow funds that includes the above (g)(6) restrictions. Simply leaving the funds with the settlement attorney, title company or putting in a bank trust account, or giving the funds to another third party does not meet the requirements for the safe harbor. The written agreement must be in place before settlement of the first relinquished property.

b. The use of a Qualified Intermediary. (see Section 6)

c. The exchangor may be entitled to interest or a growth factor on the funds held in escrow at the end of the exchange period. The interest is treated as normal interest income regardless of whether it is paid to the taxpayer in cash or is used toward the purchase of the replacement property.

d. The use of a security or guarantee arrangement, including a mortgage or third party guarantee.

5. DEFINITION OF A DISQUALIFIED PERSON. A disqualified person **may not hold the escrow account, receive identification notice, or serve as a qualified intermediary.**
Basically a disqualified person is:

a. an agent of the taxpayer at the time of the transaction. A person is considered an agent who has acted as the taxpayer's employee, **attorney**, accountant, investment broker, or real estate agent or broker within the two year period ending on the date of transfer of the first relinquished property.

> **Note:** Not considered an agent is a person who performs exchange services; or a financial institute, or title company that provides routine financial, title insurance, escrow or trust services.

b. all family members and related parties. This includes brothers and sisters, half-brothers and sisters, spouse, ancestors (parents, grandparents, etc.), and lineal descendants (children, grandchildren, etc.). In-laws are not included. A related party also includes corporations, partnerships, and trusts in which the exchangor or a disqualified party have a greater then 10% interest.

c. the person and the exchangor, and/or the person and the exchangor's agent "bear a relationship described in either section 267(b) or section 707(b) — determined by substituting in each section '10 percent' for '50 percent' each place it appears".

> **Warning:** If a totally independent person is not being utilized to insure proper control of the escrow funds, serve as Qualified Intermediary, or to receive identification

notice—the exchangor should seek legal review of Section 1.1031(k)-1(k) to be certain a "disqualified person" is not involved.

6. RECEIPT OF FUNDS BY THE EXCHANGOR. The exchangor **"may receive money or other property directly from a party to the transaction"**—but not from the qualified intermediary, qualified escrow account or trust. If the exchangor wishes to receive cash (partial tax-free exchange) then these funds should be received directly from the settlement agent and the balance of the proceeds forwarded directly to the Qualified Intermediary for placement in the Qualified Escrow Account. Otherwise the exchangor may not receive cash until the end of the 180 day exchange period or they have received all the property to which they are entitled.

7. PAYMENT OF DEPOSIT BY QUALIFIED INTERMEDIARY. Once the contract on the replacement property has been **assigned** to the Qualified Intermediary they may use the funds in the qualified escrow account to pay the earnest money deposit, make progress payments, or pay toward the down payment and the other expenditures required by the contract for the purchase and settlement of the replacement property. If the exchangor has left an earnest money deposit with the broker or settlement agent it may be returned to the exchangor after the contract has been assigned to the qualified intermediary. The payment made from the qualified escrow account must be made to the party holding the deposit, and not be made directly to the exchangor.

8. TRANSACTIONAL ITEMS. The settlement agent or the qualified intermediary may pay certain costs related to the disposition of the relinquished property and acquisition of the replacement property. These expenses are called **transactional items** and the regulation provides that they will be disregarded in determining if the exchangor is in receipt of qualified escrow funds and thus the safe harbor no longer exists.

Specifically, Section 1.1031(k)-1(g)(7)(ii) of the regulation states that the exchangor's receipt of or right to receive any of the following will be disregarded relative to the restriction on use of escrow funds—

> "(ii) Transactional items that relate to the disposition of the relinquished property or to the acquisition of the replacement property and appear under local standards in the typical closing statements as the responsibility of a buyer or seller (e.g., commissions, prorated taxes, recording or transfer taxes, and title company fees)."

In some areas of the country all settlement expenses are not normally shown on the settlement statement. For example – attorney fees are paid outside of closing. If this is the local practice then the exchangor may have to pay these expenses separately in order to stay in strict compliance with the regulation.

While similar, transactional items should not be confused with **exchange expenses**. Exchange expenses are used to determine tax wise the gain or loss realized, gain recognized, and the basis of the replacement property. See IRS Publication 544 and Section 9 of this workbook for the definition and use of exchange expenses.

Identification and Exchange Period

1. TIME LIMITS. As an outgrowth of the Starker cases the Tax Reform Act of 1984 established two time limits which are very important and require strict compliance. These are:

a. The replacement property or properties to be acquired in the exchange <u>must be identified</u> before the end of the <u>identification period.</u>

"The identification period begins on the date the taxpayer transfers the relinquished property and ends at midnight on the 45th day thereafter."

b. The identified replacement property <u>must be received</u> by the end of the <u>exchange period</u>.

"The exchange period begins on the date the taxpayer transfers the relinquished property and ends at midnight on the earlier of the 180th day thereafter or the due date(including extensions) for the taxpayer's return"

The time starts for both the identification and exchange periods when the first property being relinquished is transferred.

TIME LIMITS

<u>TRANSFER OF FIRST RELINQUISHED PROPERTY</u>

<u>TRANSFER OF REPLACEMENT PROPERTY</u>

45 DAYS
I.D. PERIOD

180 DAYS*
EXCHANGE PERIOD

---

* The earlier of 180 days or the due date (including extensions) of tax return for tax year transfer of relinquished property occurs.

2. ON TIME EXTENSION. Since the replacement property must be settled within 180 days or the tax return due date, whichever is earlier, if the exchange property being relinquished settles late in the year then it may be necessary for the exchangor to file an <u>on time</u> extension to August 15. File IRS Form 4868 to receive the automatic extension for filing of the required federal tax return.

Example: the relinquished property settles on December 15, 2004 and the tax return for 2004 is due on April 15, 2005. This would not give the exchangor the full 180 days to get to settlement on the replacement property. By filing an on time extension the exchangor could then get the full 180 days from settlement of the relinquished property to complete the exchange.

3. IDENTIFICATION RULES. While no specific rules were set forth in the 1984 Act as to how the identification was to be made, the IRS regulations published in 1991 provide specific guidance on how to identify replacement properties.

a. The identification of possible replacement properties should be as unambiguous as possible, contained in a written document or agreement, signed by the exchangor and hand delivered, mailed, telecopied, or otherwise sent before the end of the identification period.

A form letter for the exchangor to identify replacement properties is normally provided by the Qualified Intermediary after settlement of the first relinquished property. See page 5-5 for sample 45 Day Identification Letter.

The identification document is normally sent to the qualified intermediary. However it can be sent to either—the person obligated to transfer the replacement property to the exchangor, or any other person involved in the exchange other than the exchangor or a disqualified person.

The written identification may be a separate document or contained in the actual contract/agreement for the replacement property.

For real property, unambiguous identification is generally taken to mean street address, legal description, or distinguishable building name.

Important: Any replacement property actually received before the end of the identification period will be considered as identified.

b. The exchangor may identify more than one replacement property. However, regardless of the number of relinquished properties transferred by the exchangor as part of the same deferred exchange, the maximum number of replacement properties that may be identified is:

(1) three properties of any fair market value (FMV), **OR**

(2) any number of properties provided fair market value of identified properties, at end of identification period, does not exceed 200% of fair market value of all relinquished properties.

c. Identification may be revoked in writing anytime during the 45 day identification period and new properties identified.

d. If at the end of the identification period, the taxpayer has identified more properties than permitted, the taxpayer will be treated as if no replacement property has been identified. Exceptions: Any replacement property received before the end of the identification period will be considered identified; and any properties properly identified and received before the end of the exchange period which equal to at least 95% of all identified properties will be considered identified.

e. Incidental property is disregarded in the identification if in a commercial transaction it is typically transferred with the larger property and the aggregate fair market value of the incidental property does not exceed 15% of the FMV of the larger property.

Important: When after the identification is made the replacement property will be constructed or improved, OR the exchangor will be only purchasing a partial interest in the replacement property the following special identification rules apply.

4. IDENTIFICATION OF PROPERTY TO BE BUILT. The regulations provide special rules for the identification and receipt of replacement property to be built. These special rules apply when identification of a replacement property is made — and **before receipt of the property** — it will be in whole or part constructed, built, installed, manufactured, developed or improved.

The identification requirement for the property to be built will be met if the identification provides "a legal description for the underlying land and as much detail is provided regarding construction of the improvements as is practicable at the time the identification is made.

> **Note: Improvements to be made to property already owned by the exchangor are not considered like kind (see page 8–6).**

5. IDENTIFICATION OF A PARTIAL INTEREST. When an exchangor plans to purchase a partial interest in a replacement property, the 45 day identification must show the share to be purchased by the exchangor (example: a 40% interest in 123 Baker Street, Any Town, NC).

6. WHEN DOES THE TRANSFER OR RECEIPT OF PROPERTY OCCUR? The beginning of the 45 day identification period and the 180 day exchange period are both triggered by the "transfer" of the first relinquished property. For Federal income tax purposes ownership of real property occurs upon the transfer of the "benefits and burdens" of ownership.

The following are several factors that are considered in determining if ownership has transferred.

> (1) whether legal title passed; (2) how the parties treat the transaction; (3) whether an equity was acquired in the property; (4) whether the contract creates a present obligation on the seller to execute and deliver a deed and a present obligation on the purchaser to make payments; (5) whether the right of possession is vested in the purchaser; (6) which party pays the property taxes; (7) which party bears the risk of loss or damage to the property; and (8) which party receives the profits from the operation and sale of the property. [From Chapter 6, *"Tax-Free Exchanges Under Section 1031"*, by Jerry Long and Mary Foster.]

Most often we use the settlement date on the Settlement Statement (HUD-1) as the "transfer" date. Unfortunately, this date is often earlier than the actual transfer date due to a last minute delay in settlement. Exchangors should always check their settlement statement and their 45 and 180 day suspense dates to be sure they reflect the proper "transfer" date.

7. EXTENSION FOR PRESIDENTIAL DECLARED DISASTERS. The IRS announced in IRS Notice 2005-3; 2005-5 I.R.B., January 31, 2005 that Revenue Procedure 2004-13 (2004-4 I.R.B., January 26, 2004) will be retroactively modified to (1) add a minimum 120-day deadline extension for exchangors, (2) add for the extension of 'reverse exchange' deadlines, and (3) add to the conditions and categories which will qualify the like-kind exchangor for deadline extensions. The new provisions are retroactive to January 26, 2004.

When there is a presidentially declared disaster, the IRS issues a News Release. The News Release list the area affected, the extension period, and the disaster designation. For example: a News Release, dated January 26, 2005 identified as a Presidential disaster area the 62 counties in Indiana that were struck by severe winter storms and flooding. The extension period was January 1, 2005 to March 25, 2005.

The provisions added are: (1) In addition to the current extension of the 45 day identification date and the 180-day exchange period suspense dates, the four time-sensitive suspense dates for a 'reverse exchange' are now included. These dates are the 5-day period to enter into a QEAA, the 45 day identification period for the relinquished property, the 180-day EAT holding period, and the 180 day-combined period. (2) Regardless of the last extension date provided in the News Release, the exchangor will have a 120-day extension from the last day of the 45-day identification period, the 180 day exchange period, and the four reverse exchange suspense dates. The new 120-day extension date or the last day of the extension period in the News Release, whichever is later, will apply. (3) An affected exchangor now qualifies for a postponement: (a) only if the relinquished property was transferred on or before the date of the Presidentially declared disaster, or the transfer to the EAT in a 'reverse exchange', and (b) the exchangor has difficulty meeting the exchange deadlines because the relinquished or the replacement property is located in the disaster area; the principal place of business of any party to the transaction (for example, a QI, EAT, transferee, settlement agent, lender, or title insurance company) is located in the disaster area; any party to the transaction (or an employee involved in the 1031 transaction) is killed, injured or missing as a result of the disaster; a document prepared in connection with the exchange or a relevant land record is destroyed, damaged, or lost as a result of the disaster; a lender decides not to fund the loan, or is unable to due to the lack of flood, disaster or hazard insurance; or a title insurance company cannot provide a policy due to the disaster. (4) The 120 day extension described in (2) above will also apply if an already identified replacement property or an identified 'reverse exchange' relinquished property is substantially damaged by the disaster.

SAMPLE
45 DAY IDENTIFICATION LETTER

Subject: Identification of Deferred Exchange Replacement Properties

To: Realty Exchange Corporation, Qualified Intermediary
                4500 Martinwood Drive
                Haymarket, VA 20169

This letter designates and identifies those replacement properties that may be acquired as part of a tax deferred exchange under Section 1.1031 (k)-1 of the IRS Regulations and in accordance with the Exchange and Escrow Account Agreement with Realty Exchange Corporation as the Qualified Intermediary.

These properties are identified within the required 45 days following transfer of the first relinquished exchange property.

The following properties are hereby identified:

Address: _____
_____

and/ or legal description: _____
_____

Address: _____
_____

and/ or legal description: _____
_____

Address: _____
_____

and/ or legal description: _____
_____

Signed this _____ day of _____ 20_____.

_____

Exchangor's Signature

_____

Exchangor's Signature

Note: If replacement property is to be built provide as part of the identification – **a legal description** of the underlying land and **attach as much detai**l "regarding construction of the improvements as is practicable at the time the identification is made". If a partial interest is to be purchased, the identification must show the percentage of interest that may be purchased.

Section **6**

The Tax Deferred Exchange Process

1. TAX DEFERRED EXCHANGE. This type of exchange — often called a delayed or Starker Exchange — is the exchange process set forth in the IRS regulations. For the investor and the real estate broker the regulations provide a simplified process which fits in very nicely with normal day to day real estate operations. This process permits the normal Realtor® listing and purchase contract process to work for all parties involved.

It provides time to sell the exchangor's property, to locate and place under contract a new property and to go to settlement in an orderly fashion. By using a Qualified Intermediary the exchangor is not dependent on the buyer or seller agreeing to be involved in the process.

2. USE OF QUALIFIED INTERMEDIARY. For the "Safe Harbor" provisions of the Section 1031 regulations to apply an exchangor must use a Qualified Intermediary in a tax deferred exchange. Normally the Qualified Intermediary is referred by the owner's real estate agent, accountant, attorney or the settlement agent. A list of Qualified Intermediaries who are members of the Federation of Exchange Accommodators (FEA) can be found on the Federation's web site www.1031.org. Also those individuals who have demonstrated through experience and rigorous testing their knowledge of the Like Kind exchange process and rules have been designated by the FEA as *Certified Exchange Specialist*. A roster of CES designees can be found at www.1031ces.org.

IRS defines a Qualified Intermediary as:

> "a person who is not the taxpayer or a disqualified person, and enters into a written agreement with the taxpayer and, as required by the exchange agreement, acquires the relinquished property from the taxpayer, transfers the relinquished property, acquires the replacement property, and transfers the replacement property to the taxpayer".

3. THE EXCHANGE PROCESS. The process starts with the listing of the property being relinquished. After the exchangor has a contract on the relinquished property and provides a copy to the Qualified Intermediary, the process is simply for the Qualified Intermediary — which is most often a corporation set-up specifically to do exchanges — to prepare the exchange and escrow account agreement which outlines each step in the exchange process. Normally the exchange agreement is prepared and signed after there is a ratified contract on the property to be relinquished.

SEE CHART ON PAGE 6–3

Also prior to settlement the Qualified Intermediary is **assigned** the purchase contract for the relinquished property (see Appendix A for sample Assignment of Contract). The regulations also require that the assignment of the contract to the intermediary be in writing and that all parties to the contract be notified of the assignment on or before settlement (see Appendix A for sample Notification of Assignment).

Important. The agreement and the assignment must be signed, and the Notification of Assignment made prior to the settlement of the relinquished property.

At settlement, the property being relinquished is transferred from the exchangor to the Qualified Intermediary. Immediately the Qualified Intermediary transfers the property to the Buyer — and in turn receives the funds from the Buyer. These proceeds or Exchange escrow funds are placed in qualified escrow account by the Qualified Intermediary so that the exchangor has no control over them.

The qualified intermediary remains an important player in the exchange for the purchase of the new replacement properties. When the new properties are located and identified, and the contract terms accepted, the exchangor assigns the contract to the Qualified Intermediary. At settlement the Qualified Intermediary provides the settlement agent the necessary funds from the Qualified Escrow Account

In turn, the Qualified Intermediary transfers the property to the exchangor and the exchange is accomplished. After disbursing any remaining funds, providing a final accounting of the escrow funds, and forwarding any interest, the role of the Qualified Intermediary is complete.

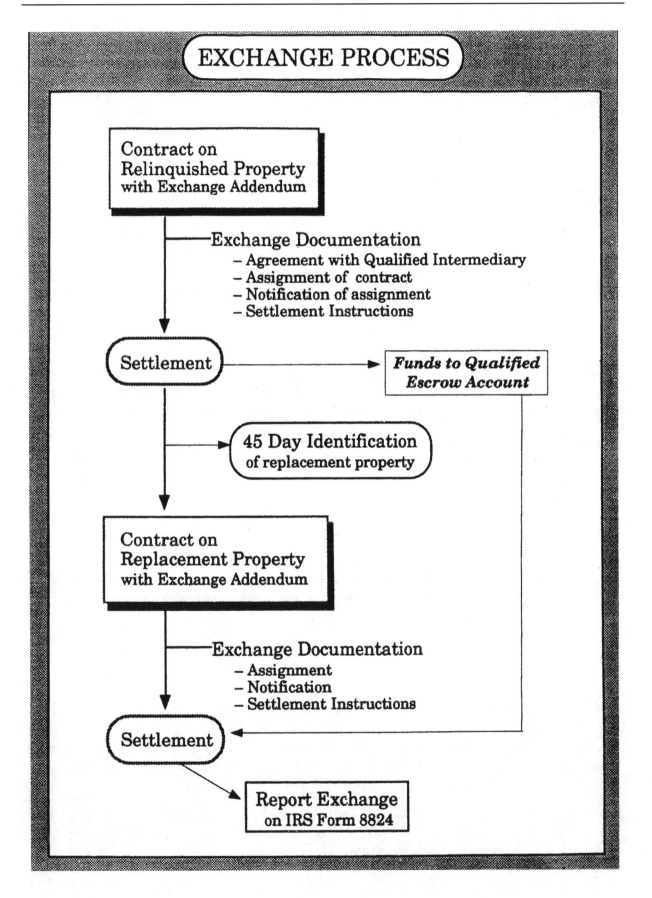

EXCHANGE PROCESS

Contract on Relinquished Property with Exchange Addendum

Exchange Documentation
- Agreement with Qualified Intermediary
- Assignment of contract
- Notification of assignment
- Settlement Instructions

Settlement → *Funds to Qualified Escrow Account*

45 Day Identification of replacement property

Contract on Replacement Property with Exchange Addendum

Exchange Documentation
- Assignment
- Notification
- Settlement Instructions

Settlement

Report Exchange on IRS Form 8824

4. CONTRACT TO PURCHASE THE RELINQUISHED PROPERTY. As with all listings it is the objective to get a Contract as soon as possible. It is not important in this type exchange if the buyers are investors or plan to use the property as a principal residence. When the contract is presented it will most likely be on a standard Realtor® or company form. It is thus recommended to add the following type statement as an addendum to the standard contract for purchase of the exchangor's property (see page A–7 in Appendix A for sample Addendum):

> Notwithstanding anything in this purchase agreement to the contrary, it is the intent of the Owner/Exchangor to transfer the property to the Purchaser as part of a Tax Deferred Like-Kind Exchange.
>
> It is the intent of the parties that the Owner/Exchangor be allowed to use Section 1031 of the Internal Revenue Code to exchange this property for other replacement property to be identified and acquired later in accordance with Section 1031 regulations.
>
> This contract may be assigned to a qualified intermediary solely for the purpose of completing the exchange. The purchaser will be notified in writing when this assignment is made. Title, however, will be conveyed directly from the Owner/ Exchangor to the Purchaser as authorized by Revenue Ruling 90-34.
>
> The Purchaser will be held harmless, and no additional expense or liability will be incurred by the Purchaser as a result of this like-kind exchange. All other items and conditions of this contract remain in full force and effect.

Listing agents may also wish to include in the contract a statement that the exchangor acknowledges they have received independent professional advice regarding the like kind exchange and are not relying on the Realtor® for advice.

The purpose of this addendum is threefold: first, to show owner's intent to do an exchange; second, to permit assignment of the contract to the Qualified Intermediary, as many standard contracts do not permit assignment without agreement; third, to ensure the buyers that there is no additional expense or liability on their part. If the contract is 'quiet' on assignment, then the contract may be assigned without the use of any addendum.

It is important to stress that after the Purchasers sign the initial Exchange Addendum there is no requirement for them to sign any other documents relative to the exchange.

With the ratification of the contract to purchase the property being relinquished, the Exchange process is in full swing. The next step is for the Qualified Intermediary to prepare the exchange and escrow account agreement.

5. ADVANCE PREPARATION OF EXCHANGE DOCUMENTATION. The most desirable method for handling exchange documentation is to have it completed and signed by the exchangor and Qualified Intermediary prior to settlement. Unfortunately some Qualified Intermediaries send the exchange documentation to the settlement agent/ attorney to have signed at settlement. Some of the many advantages to having the documentation signed in advance are:

a. The exchangor/ seller is confident that all the required documents for the exchange to take place have been completed. Too often an exchangor will show up at settlement thinking an exchange will take place and nothing has been done in advance.

b. No additional action is required at closing by the settlement agent/ attorney. No documents pertaining to the exchange need to be signed.

c. The Qualified Intermediary can answer any questions the exchangor has about the exchange documentation or process in advance of settlement. Normally the settlement agent/ attorney is not willing or is not qualified to answer questions at the settlement table.

d. There is less confusion and stress at settlement for both the buyer and seller when all the exchange documents have been signed in advance.

6. ACQUIRING REPLACEMENT PROPERTY. When the exchangor's property is listed, the owners should begin planning on what type property or properties they desire to obtain. We have learned that the property to be obtained must be "like kind"—but we have also learned that a great number and different type of properties will meet that criteria. The exchangors should decide what type of new property is desired, the location, the purchase price, the cash down payment, type financing, negative cash flow that can be handled, etc., before the search for replacement properties is started and the 45 day identification made.

If the replacement property desired is being constructed or will require new financing, the time limits can become a factor. Anytime new financing is involved the lender needs to be identified early and be made aware of the exchange transaction to insure there are no underwriting problems.

7. REPLACEMENT PROPERTY CONTRACT ADDENDUM. When the replacement property is located and the price, loan terms, etc. are accepted, it is recommended that the following be added as an addendum to the standard purchase contract.

> The Purchaser/Exchangor is acquiring this property to complete a Like-Kind Deferred Exchange under Section 1031 of the Internal Revenue Code.
>
> Solely for the purpose of completing the Exchange this contract may be assigned to the qualified intermediary. The seller will be notified in writing when this assignment is made. Title, however, shall be conveyed directly from the Seller to the Exchangor in accordance with Revenue Ruling 90-34.
>
> Seller will be held harmless and there will be no additional expense to the Seller as a result of this Like-Kind Exchange.

NOTE: A contract may be written on a replacement property prior to the settlement of the relinquished property. However, the replacement property may not be transferred prior to settlement of the relinquished property.

8. TRANSFER OF PROPERTY INVOLVING A QUALIFIED INTERMEDIARY. In accordance with the required Exchange Agreement, the Qualified Intermediary acquires the relinquished property from the exchangor, transfers the relinquished property to the buyer, acquires the replacement property, and transfers replacement property to the exchangor.

There are two methods set forth in the regulations (§1.1031(k)–1(g)(4)(iv)) as to how the Qualified Intermediary can acquire and transfer property. These are:

a. the Qualified Intermediary acquires and transfers **legal title** to that property, or

b. the Qualified Intermediary **enters into a contract agreement** with the buyer to transfer the relinquished property to the buyer; and the Qualified Intermediary enters into a contract agreement with the seller to transfer the replacement property to the exchangor; and the properties are transferred in accordance with the agreements.

The regulation provides a very simple method for the Qualified Intermediary to enter into the contract agreements. The regulation states:

> an intermediary is treated as entering into an agreement if **the rights** of a party (exchangor) to the agreement **are assigned** to the intermediary and **all parties** to the agreement **are notified** in writing of the assignment on or before the date of the relevant transfer of the property.

This clearly sets forth the requirement to assign the contracts signed by the exchangor to the qualified intermediary and to notify all of the parties to the contract of the assignment.

9. SETTLEMENT INSTRUCTIONS. In the Tax Deferred Exchange process one of the important steps for the Qualified Intermediary is to provide exchange settlement instructions to the settlement agent (also known as the escrow agent, settlement attorney, or closing agent). Each Qualified Intermediary has their own format for providing instructions as there is no specific guidance in the regulations. The primary objective is to have the Settlement Statement (HUD-1) reflect in fact that the transaction is an exchange.

The instructions to the settlement agent include such items as showing the property being transferred through the Qualified Intermediary, the direct wire transfer of all exchange escrow funds (proceeds) to the Qualified Intermediary, and deeding instructions (see HUD-1 example in Appendix A).

10. TRANSFER OF TITLE. In April 1990 the IRS Revenue Ruling 90-34 authorized the use of a Direct Deed if all actions made the transaction an exchange. As a result, almost all exchanges using a Qualified Intermediary use the Direct Deed to transfer title. This keeps the Qualified Intermediary from being in the title chain and reduces their liability.

A Direct Deed transfers the title to the property directly from one party to the other without the third party in the exchange ever being shown in the deed. This means that the Exchangor, as the owner of the relinquished property, deeds the property directly to the buyer, and the seller of the replacement property deeds the property directly to the Exchangor as the purchaser.

11. CONTINUITY OF TITLE. The exchangor's interest in the replacement property should be titled **in the same name(s) and tax I.D. number** as was used with the relinquished property. There are three "disregarded entity" exceptions to this rule. They are:

a. a revocable trust. As a disregarded entity title to the replacement property may be taken in the name of the revocable trust.

b. a disregarded entity single member LLC. Only in community property states may a husband and wife both be members of the LLC. If necessary in other states both the husband and wife can created a single member LLC.

c. Delaware Statutory Trust (DST). IRS Revenue Ruling 2004-86 provides that under certain circumstances as described in the revenue ruling a DST will be treated as a disregarded entity for federal income tax purposes. Thus the taxpayer may exchange real property for an interest in the Delaware Statutory Trust. The beneficial owners of a DST are provided the same liability protection as shareholders in a Delaware corporation. This exception is important to sponsors and purchasers of tenant-in-common (TIC) exchange properties.

Important. The exchangor should immediately contact their Qualified Intermediary if there is any intention to take title in any form other then as the relinquished property was titled.

12. PURCHASE OF LLC AS REPLACEMENT PROPERTY. A number of Private Letter Rulings have established that when an LLC owns the replacement property as its sole asset, the exchangor can purchase the LLC as the replacement property. This avoids the real estate transfer tax on the replacement property. The exchangor must hold the LLC as a single owner electing to be disregarded as a separate entity.

13. DEFERRED EXCHANGE CHECKLIST. With the IRS regulations there is a very logical sequence of steps to be followed by the exchangors, their attorney and real estate agent to be certain that the exchange meets the IRS requirements for a tax deferred exchange. To assist with this process a Checklist and Documentation worksheet is included in Appendix A.

14. CERTIFICATION OF FUNDS. The exchangor has no control of the funds so the certification of the availability of funds for the down payment or to support a loan application must come from the Qualified Intermediary holding the Escrow funds.

15. DIRECT SIMULTANEOUS EXCHANGE WITH A QUALIFIED INTERMEDIARY. We most often relate the use of a qualified intermediary with an exchange when there is a delay between settlements. However, even when the settlements are simultaneous, the buyers and sellers most often do not desire to participate as accommodators. Thus the exchangor uses a qualified intermediary to prepare the required documentation and to affect the transfer of the property. The IRS regulations give specific approval to the use of the qualified intermediary in a simultaneous exchange. A simultaneous exchange occurs when the seller is transferring the relinquished property and receiving the replacement property from the same party. If the seller as an exchangor is transferring the relinquished property to one party and receiving the replacement property from a different party, even if on the same day, it is not a simultaneous exchange, but a tax deferred exchange requiring a Qualified Intermediary.

16. EXCHANGE FEES. Each Qualified Intermediary is going to have their own schedule of fees. However, for planning purposes approximately $1,000 should be used as the fee for preparation of the documentation, securing the escrow funds, and acting as a Qualified Intermediary. A sample Qualified Intermediary fee schedule is contained in Appendix A.

The QI fee does not include normal settlement and recording fees paid to the settlement agent. Also separate are fees for legal or accounting advice obtained by the exchangor. The regulations permit the taxpayer to be paid interest or a growth factor by the holder of the exchange escrow funds. This payment upon completion of the exchange is treated as interest and reported as such by the taxpayer. By regulation the interest paid is for the period between transfer of the first relinquished property and receipt of the final replacement property. Some qualified intermediaries charge a lower exchange fee but keep the interest earned on the exchange funds being held. A taxpayer should be certain of all of the fees to be charged, and if interest will be paid on the exchange funds to be held.

17. FIDELITY BOND. Since the security of the exchange escrow being held by a QI is of paramount importance to the exchangor, members of the Federation of Exchange Accommodators (FEA) may

obtain fidelity bond insurance issued by insurance giant CNA. This insurance covers losses attributable to both QI employees and owners. For example, Realty Exchange Corporation carries a $5 million dollar per occurrence fidelity bond. Thus exchangors can be certain their exchange escrow funds will be secure and available when the time comes to purchase their replacement property. In addition to the fees to be charged a taxpayer should check to see if the Qualified Intermediary is bonded.

18. COMPLIANCE WITH FIRPTA. If the seller in an exchange transaction, including the Exchangor, is a nonresident alien or foreign corporation the reporting and withholding requirements of the Foreign Investment in Real Property Tax Act of 1980 (FIRPTA) must be followed. Green card holders are not nonresident aliens and may do an exchange without federal withholding. If the seller (transferor) is a foreign person or corporation the buyer (transferee) must withhold and forward to the IRS 10% of the sales price. If a non-resident alien or foreign corporation is doing an exchange they may submit a request to the IRS to obtain a waiver of withholding.

19. EARNEST MONEY DEPOSIT ON REPLACEMENT PROPERTY. Since it is customary that the exchangor/purchaser give some type of earnest money deposit when they make a contract offer on the replacement property, the question how to handle the deposit comes up in almost every exchange. Three common situations are:

First, if the exchangor is going to have to bring cash to the settlement, over and above the amount in escrow, then the exchangor should make the deposit and have that amount credited at settlement toward purchase of the replacement property.

Second, when the contract on the replacement property is written before the closing on the relinquished property, the exchangor normally makes the deposit with the contract offer. Later, if desired, after the closing of the relinquished property, the Qualified Intermediary may substitute the cash deposit.

Third, when the replacement property contract is written after the Qualified Intermediary is holding the escrow funds the exchangor has four options:

(1) make a cash deposit and let it ride toward the purchase price;
(2) make the required cash deposit and request the Qualified Intermediary replace it with a substitute deposit;
(3) make a small cash deposit and agree in the contract for an additional deposit to be made by the Qualified Intermediary in 7 to 10 working days; or
(4) give the seller a promissory note with the provision that the Qualified Intermediary will pay it off within 7 to 10 working days after ratification of the contract.

If the Qualified Intermediary is to replace the deposit, add to the deposit, or payoff the Note then the following must happen:

(1) a copy of the contract must be provided to the Qualified Intermediary;
(2) the Qualified Intermediary prepares the Assignment of Replacement Property Contract and it is signed and returned to the Qualified Intermediary by the Exchangor; and
(3) the Qualified Intermediary forwards the required deposit to the party named in the contract and requests, if applicable, the deposit made by the exchangor be returned to them.

Tax wise it makes no difference if the exchangor makes a cash deposit and then after settlement of the final replacement property receives that amount in cash from the settlement agent or from the

Qualified Intermediary. Because — in an exchange — 'cash in offsets cash out'.

Important. No deposit may be made by the Qualified Intermediary until the exchangor's interest in the contract is assigned by the exchangor to the Qualified Intermediary.

Notes

New Basis – Depreciation – Installment Sale Shared Equity – TIC Properties – Private Annuity Trust

1. BASIS IN NEW PROPERTIES. When an investor buys a new property the basis is normally the purchase price plus some acquisition costs. However, in the case of an exchange determining the basis in the new properties requires an additional step.

Let us say we purchased two replacement properties that had an acquisition cost of $400,000 and $200,000 – for a total of $600,000.

The easy method to determine the total basis in the new properties is to subtract from the acquisition cost the realized gain deferred.

$600,000	ACQUISITION COSTS OF NEW PROPERTIES
- 355,000	less: REALIZED GAIN DEFERRED
$245,000	TOTAL NEW BASIS

2. DEPRECIATION. We need the new basis for the replacement properties to set up our depreciation schedule. To determine the depreciation schedule for each new property we allocate basis to the properties in the ratio of their relative market value.

	MARKET VALUE	RATIO
Exchange Property #1	$400,000	67%
Exchange Property #2	200,000	33%
Total	$600,000	100%

The new depreciation schedule for analysis purposes will then be computed as follows:

	EXCHANGE #1	PROPERTY #2
Allocation	67%	33%
New Basis	$164,150	$80,850
($245,000)	– 32,820	–16,170
Less: Land (20%)	131,330	64,680
Improvements	4,775	2,352
Annual Depreciation (27.5 Years – S.L.)*		

*If the property was nonresidential the depreciation would be straight line for 39 years. See below for new depreciation method for replacement properties.

3. DEPRECIATION OF REPLACEMENT PROPERTY. In January 2000 IRS Notice 2000-4 provided guidance on how to depreciate like kind exchange replacement property. In February 2004 the IRS released temporary and proposed regulations on the topic. In Notice 2000-4 the IRS favorably changed the way new replacement property was to be depreciated. Under the new regulation (T.D. 9115) the general rule remains that the taxpayer must depreciate the remaining relinquished property adjusted basis over the remaining recovery period using the same depreciation method as if it were a continuation of the relinquished property depreciation schedule. Any increase in the basis will be treated as newly acquired property and will be depreciated over 27.5 or 39 years using a new separate straight line depreciation schedule.

> **Example:** An exchangor has been taking depreciation for 10 years on a residential rental with $150,000 of depreciable improvements. Each year he took $5,454 of straight line depreciation ($150,000 ÷ 27.5) for a total of $54,545.
>
> Now he will continue to depreciate the new replacement property by $5,454 per year for the next 17.5 years until the $95,445 remaining depreciation is taken ($150,000 – 54,545), while at the same time he will take depreciation on the balance of the replacement property depreciable improvements above the

$95,445 carried forward using a new 27.5 or 39 year schedule.

The new regulation does permit the taxpayer to **elect out of the rules** and to treat the entire replacement property as a new asset. The new regulation applies to exchanges completed after February 27, 2004. For complete details search for T.D. 9115 at www.irs.gov.

4. INSTALLMENT SALE. Often an Exchangor must take back a Note from the buyer in order to dispose of the relinquished property. In April 1994 the IRS amended the 1031 regulations (§1.1031(k)-1(j)), coordinating the deferred like-kind exchange and installment sale rules. The regulations provide that:

(1) A Note received from the Qualified Intermediary and not directly from the buyer of the relinquished property **may receive installment sale treatment**.

(2) If the Exchangor receives cash from the Qualified Intermediary at the end of the exchange or if the Exchangor has a bona fide intent to do an exchange, but does not complete the exchange by receiving a replacement property, then **the gain due will be reported for the tax year in which the Exchangor actually receives the cash from the Qualified Intermediary**.

> **Example:** The Exchangor relinquishes a debt free property on December 15, 2004 for $100,000. The Qualified Intermediary receives $80,000 in cash and a Note from the buyer for $20,000. The Exchangor identifies a single replacement property and goes to settlement on the purchase on March 30, 2005. However, the Exchangor only uses $60,000 of the cash in escrow to purchase the replacement property. Following settlement, the Qualified Intermediary returns to the Exchangor $20,000 (cash boot) and endorses the $20,000 Note (non-like kind property boot) over to the Exchangor. The cash and the value of the Note received will be recognized as capital gain by the Exchangor on his tax return for 2005, not on the 2004 return when the property was actually relinquished and the Qualified Intermediary received the cash and Note from the buyer. Even if the Exchangor does not complete the exchange by obtaining a replacement property — if there was a bona fide intent to exchange — then the gain will still be reported on an installment basis for the tax year the cash was received from the Qualified Intermediary.

5. TREATMENT OF A NOTE FROM BUYER. In an exchange which involves a Note being given by the buyer of the relinquished property, two different approaches may be taken, these are:

One, at settlement the Exchangor receives the Note directly from the buyer. The value of the Note becomes taxable income as non-like property and may be treated as an installment sale.

Two, at settlement the Qualified Intermediary receives the Note directly from the buyer. That is, the Note is made payable to the Qualified Intermediary. The Note then becomes part of the qualified escrow held by the Qualified Intermediary and can be disposed of as follows:

> a. The Qualified Intermediary can sell the Note, usually at a discount, and add the proceeds to the other cash in the qualified escrow account (no boot to Exchangor), or

> b. The Note can be use as part of the compensation for the purchase of the replacement property (no boot to Exchangor). At settlement the Note is endorsed to the seller of the replacement property by the Qualified Intermediary; or

> c. If the Note matures in less than 180 days, the Qualified Intermediary places the payoff in the qualified escrow account, and uses the funds toward purchase of the replacement property; or

d. At settlement of the replacement property, the exchangor can purchase the Note from the Qualified Intermediary. The cash received is used toward the purchase of the replacement property; or

e. After the exchange, the Note is endorsed by the Qualified Intermediary to the Exchangor and the Note can be reported as an installment sale.

Note: While holding the Note the Qualified Intermediary must collect interest and comply with all other provisions set forth in the Note.

6. SHARED EQUITY FINANCING AGREEMENT.
The personal use of a home by a co-owner may disqualify the property as an investment property unless there is a "shared equity financing agreement". If the exchangor plans to purchase with a co-owner a replacement property in which the co-owner will live, it is essential that they have a written Shared Equity Financing Agreement.

Otherwise, without this Agreement, the IRS will treat the property as a personal use second home. As such, it will not qualify as a rental or an exchange replacement property. Most real estate professionals are not familiar with this requirement and few attorneys are able to prepare the Agreement. Thus, if you are planning to co-own your investment property with an occupant, we strongly recommend you obtain from Amazon.com the book "The New Home Buying Strategy" by Attorney Marilyn D. Sullivan. This book will help you prepare the Agreement.

7. TENANCY-IN-COMMON.
In an exchange the taxpayer must be able to take title to a specific interest in the property (that is, the taxpayer must be on the deed). For example, purchasing an interest in a partnership does not qualify. Thus, many properties involving co-owners are purchased as "tenants-in-common" with each co-owner on the deed.

There has been a need for a number of years for developers of large commercial properties to provide 1031 exchangors a way to purchase an interest in the commercial property as a tenant-in-common. In March 2002 the IRS released Revenue Procedure 2002-22 to address fractional ownership interests as replacement property in a Like Kind exchange. These are known as tenancy-in-common interests or TIC interests. As a result a number of commercial real estate companies are now offering TIC interests to exchangors in order for them to complete their Like Kind exchange.

Basically the way it works is that a real estate project sponsor owns one or more commercial properties in which they will sell a Tenancy-in-Common fractional interest to a number of co-owners. The sponsor has a Master Lease with a Management Company for a fixed monthly amount. The Master Lease is typically a triple-net lease so that the property owners need not worry about day-to-day operation of the property, do not share expenses or profits, but will receive a specific return on their equity.

The Revenue Procedure did not provide "safe harbor" provisions but authorized project sponsors to request a Private Letter Ruling on their specific offerings and listed 15 specific requirements to be met for a favorable ruling. For example: each co-owner takes title as a tenant-in-common, the number of co-owners cannot exceed 35, co-owners must unanimously agree on major decisions such as sale, lease and financing, co-owner activity is limited, revenues and expenses must be shared according to interest owned, and each co-owner retains the right to transfer, partition or encumber their interest with other co-owner approval.

Occasionally an exchangor cannot complete an exchange because: 1) they are unable to find and identify replacement property within the 45 day identification period; 2) an identified property cannot be placed under contract or the contract falls out sometime after the 45th day and the exchangor has no alternate property identified; or 3) they cannot find a desirable property for the equity, value and debt that must be replaced.

The TIC type commercial offering helps solve these problems. The great advantage is that there are a number of properties available, the size of the TIC interest and date for closing are very flexible. Normally the cash equity to be invested needs to be only least $100,000 or greater.

If within the 45 day identification period an exchangor is unable to identify a replacement property or is uncertain about the suitability of an identified replacement property, they can quickly identify a TIC property as an alternative. They will then have up to a total of 180 days to close on their interest in the TIC property and complete the exchange. As with any investment the exchangor needs to investigate the fees, return on investment and resale opportunities.

8. COMBINING A LIKE KIND EXCHANGE AND A PRIVATE ANNUITY TRUST.
Often the situation for an exchangor goes like this – "I want to sell my highly appreciated rental or investment property for $1 million and exchange for a $500,000 property." If the taxpayer were to do such an exchange, then he would have to pay capital gains tax on up to $500,000 of gain. A solution is for the taxpayer to combine a 1031 like kind exchange with a Private Annuity Trust (PAT).

In a PAT the taxpayer transfers (sells) an appreciated asset to a family controlled trust (the PAT) for an annuity contract. The PAT then sells the property and uses the proceeds to fund the annuity. The capital gain (depreciation and profit) is tax deferred until the taxpayer (annuitant) begins to receive payments.

When the taxpayer desires a lower priced replacement property for income, business, or maybe personal purposes, a like kind exchange and a private annuity trust can be combined to defer all of the capital gain taxes.

> **Caution:** The decision to use a Private Annuity Trust requires advanced planning. The Trust should be set up and the percentage to be sold to the Trust should be transferred **before there is a contract on the relinquished property.**

The steps are for the taxpayer to transfer (sell) the desired percentage of the property to the PAT. The remaining taxpayer's interest and the PAT's interest are then sold to a third party buyer. The interest still belonging to the taxpayer is transferred as part of a regular like kind exchange. At settlement the proceeds are split, with part going to the PAT and the balance to the Qualified Intermediary as Exchange Escrow Funds. The replacement property is then purchased as in a regular exchange. The funds received by the PAT are used to fund the annuity.

For a detailed explanation of a Private Annuity Trust go to www.nafep.com and select "Capital Gains tax planning".

9. A SINGLE PROPERTY CAN QUALIFY FOR BOTH EXCLUSION AND DEFERRAL OF GAIN.
IRS Revenue Procedure 2005-14, effective January 27, 2005, applies to taxpayers who exchange a single property that satisfies the requirements for both the exclusion of gain from the exchange of a principal residence under IRC Section 121, and the non-recognition of gain from the exchange of like-kind property under Section 1031.

To qualify for the principal residence exclusion of up to $250,000 of gain (up to $500,000 if married and filing jointly), the taxpayer must have owned and lived in the property for two of the last five years, but does not have to live in the property at the time of the exchange. To qualify for the Section 1031 like-kind exchange deferral of the gain, the taxpayer at the time of the exchange must be holding the property for rental, business or investment purposes, and the new replacement property must also be held for business, rental or investment purposes. The Section 121 exclusion is taken first. Any Section 1250 depreciation taken on the property after May 6, 1997 must be recaptured and may not be excluded under Section 121. However, it may be deferred under Section 1031.

If the gain on the sale of the rental property is less than the excluded amount of $250,000 or $500,000 then only the exclusion is claimed and the cash received may be used anyway the owner desires. If the gain significantly exceeds the $250,000 or $500,000 exclusion, then the owner should consider taking the exclusion and also doing a like kind exchange.

For example, John, a single taxpayer, purchased a home in January 2000 for $200,000. He made $20,000 worth of improvements and has $100,000 remaining on his mortgage. The home was his principal residence until the end of December 2003. He converted the property to a rental and has taken $20,000 in depreciation. In December 2005 he sells the property for $580,000 and has $30,000 in selling costs. The total realized gain on the sale is $350,000. The gain is determined by taking the selling price of $580,000 and subtracting the $30,000 of selling costs for an adjusted sales price of $550,000. His current tax basis of $200,000 is subtracted from the $550,000. The tax basis is figured by taking the original cost plus improvements of $220,000, and subtracting the depreciation allowed. This leaves John with a realized gain of $350,000.

Since John qualifies for the principal residence exclusion, $250,000 is subtracted from the total gain of $350,000. The balance of gain to be deferred under Section 1031 is $100,000. If John does not do an exchange, the federal tax to be paid would be $17,000. This includes $5,000 for the recapture of the depreciation and $12,000 on the balance of the capital gain. Since John owed $100,000 on the property, after paying selling costs there is $450,000 in proceeds at settlement. John may take the $250,000 value of his exclusion, tax free, in cash at settlement.

To defer the entire $100,000 of gain not excluded, John will have to purchase a replacement property as part of his exchange that costs at least $300,000. He must also invest the $200,000 of remaining proceeds as a down payment on the new property. The balance of the funds needed to purchase the replacement property may be borrowed and/or be new cash. The revenue procedure also provides guidance and examples for when on one property there are two structures. One used as a principal residence and one for business purposes. It also addresses the exchange of a single structure used partly as a personal residence and partly for business purposes (such as for a home office).

The importance of this revenue procedure is that it clearly recognizes that the sale and exchange of a single property may qualify for both the exclusion of gain under Section 121 and the deferral of gain under Section 1031. For a copy of Revenue Procedure 2005-14, go to www.irs.gov and search for I.R.B. 2005-7, Feb 14, 2005.

Reverse Exchange Procedures – Construction and To-be-built Exchanges

1. REVERSE EXCHANGE BACKGROUND. There are times when an exchangor must take title to a desired replacement property before he can transfer the property to be relinquished. This is known as a reverse exchange and is not currently allowed under the IRC 1031 Like-Kind Exchange regulations.

However, the exchange industry had for a number of years requested that the IRS establish some type of procedure to accommodate this situation. In the absence of IRS guidance exchangors were using third parties to take title to the eventual replacement property, having them own and operate the property, sometimes building improvements, until such time as the exchangor could transfer their relinquished property and purchase the replacement property from the third party owner. These are called "parking arrangements".

2. IRS REVENUE PROCEDURE 2000-37: PROCEDURES FOR THE ACCOMMODATION OF REVENUE EXCHANGES.
In September 2000 the IRS published IRS Revenue Procedure 2000-37 (see Appendix C). This Procedure establishes "safe harbor" rules to formally provide for and document such "parking arrangements". The procedure requires that the relinquished or **eventual replacement property be held by the "exchange accommodation titleholder"(EAT) in a "qualified exchange accommodation arrangement" (QEAA).**

Taxpayers and advisors should be aware that if the services of an EAT are required it can be expensive and requires strict adherence to the Revenue Procedure.

The QEAA must meet the following requirements:

(1) The exchange accommodation titleholder will have legal title to the property or "such other indicia of ownership".

(2) It is the bona fide intent of the taxpayer to do an exchange.

(3) A written Qualified Exchange Accommodation Agreement is prepared within five days of transfer of ownership to the exchange accommodation titleholder, and the written agreement provides that:

> (a) the exchange accommodation titleholder is holding the property for the benefit of the taxpayer in order to complete an exchange under Section 1031;

> (b) the exchange accommodation titleholder will be treated as the beneficial owner of the property for federal income tax purposes; and

> (c) the EAT will file federal tax returns as necessary.

(4) Within 45 days after transfer of ownership to the exchange accommodation titleholder the relinquished property must be identified. The taxpayer may identify alternate or multiple relinquished property.

(5) No later than 180 days after transfer of ownership to the exchange accommodation titleholder, the replacement property must be transferred to the taxpayer.

3. DISQUALIFIED EXCHANGE ACCOMMODATION TITLEHOLDER.
The exchange accommodation titleholder may not be the taxpayer or a disqualified party as set forth in IRS Regulation 1.1031(k)-1(k). See Paragraph 5 of Section 4 of this book. Qualified Intermediary companies have set up separate entities or have made separate working arrangements with companies that have been established to serve as an exchange accommodation titleholder.

4. PERMITTED CONTRACTUAL ARRANGEMENTS.
The following legal or contractual arrangements may be made without invalidating the Qualified Exchange Accommodation Arrangement:

> (a) The taxpayer or a disqualified person may guarantee the obligations of the exchange accommodation titleholder, including debt, or may indemnify the exchange accommodation titleholder against cost and expenses.

(b) The taxpayer or disqualified person may loan or advance funds to the exchange accommodation titleholder, or guarantee a loan or advance to the exchange accommodation titleholder.

(c) The taxpayer or disqualified person may lease the property from the exchange accommodation titleholder.

(d) The taxpayer or a disqualified person may manage the property, supervise improvement of the property, act as a contractor, or otherwise provide services to the exchange accommodation titleholder with respect to the property.

(e) The taxpayer and exchange accommodation titleholder may enter into a contract relating to the purchase or sale of the property.

(f) The exchange accommodation titleholder may also serve as the Qualified Intermediary.

5. HOW DOES THE PROCESS WORK? The Exchange Accommodation Titleholder (EAT) may take title to either the **replacement** property or the **relinquished** property.

a. **Replacement Property**. The process for the EAT to take title to the replacement property is basically as follows:

1) The taxpayer selects a QI to do the Like Kind exchange part of the transaction.

2) Taxpayer ratifies contract with current owner to purchase replacement property.

3) Taxpayer selects an EAT to purchase and hold replacement property.

   Note: Normally the EAT will be an LLC set up specifically for this transaction.

4) Taxpayer assigns replacement property contract to EAT.

5) Taxpayer and EAT sign the Qualified Exchange Accommodation Arrangement (QEAA). This agreement also serves as the contract for taxpayer to purchase replacement property from EAT. There may also be Management and Lease agreements between the taxpayer and EAT. This gives the taxpayer the authority to manage the replacement property on a day-to-day basis, and to coordinate directly with any contractors.

6) Taxpayer arranges for **financing** for EAT to purchase replacement property (usually a combination of a loan to the EAT and the guarantee of a loan to the EAT by a commercial lender).

7) EAT takes title to replacement property.

8) Taxpayer identifies relinquished property within 45 days of transfer of replacement property to EAT.

9) Taxpayer receives contract on relinquished property, and completes normal exchange documentation with QI.

10) Taxpayer/ exchangor completes settlement on relinquished property. Exchange escrow funds go to the QI.

11) If necessary, taxpayer makes normal 45 day identification of replacement property.

12) Taxpayer assigns QEAA (which includes contract to purchase replacement property) to QI.

The QI then completes normal exchange documentation for replacement property.

13) The replacement property is transferred from the EAT to the taxpayer/ exchangor. The property is purchased with the exchange escrow funds from the QI, with the assumption of the loans made to the EAT or through new financing.

   Normally transfer occurs immediately following closing on the relinquished property. Transfer may be delayed if new construction must be completed to meet the reinvestment requirements.

14) Exchangor reports exchange to IRS on Form 8824. The EAT reports the transaction to the IRS and State tax authorities.

b. **Relinquished Property**. Often, due to already established financing, it is better for the EAT to take title to the relinquished property. This then sets up a normal exchange in which the taxpayer is transferring the relinquished property before receiving the replacement property. The process for the EAT to take title to the relinquished property is as follows:

1) The taxpayer has a contract to purchase the replacement property by a certain date, and either he doesn't have a buyer for the relinquished property or the buyer cannot go to settlement before the date the replacement property must be transferred.

2) Taxpayer selects a QI and EAT to do the Like Kind exchange.

3) Taxpayer and EAT sign QEAA. This Agreement also serves as the contract for the EAT to purchase and hold the relinquished property. It may provide for the taxpayer to lease back and manage the property. The QEAA will stipulate that the EAT must transfer the relinquished property to a third party buyer within 180 days of the EAT taking title to the relinquished property.

4) The QI prepares the exchange documents for both properties with the EAT as the purchaser of the relinquished property and the taxpayer as purchaser of the replacement property.

5) Both the QEAA and the replacement property contract are assigned to the QI.

6) The EAT will purchase the relinquished property by the assumption of any existing loans and by borrowing from the taxpayer the cash equity in the property.

7) To purchase the replacement property the taxpayer must use his own funds and/ or arrange new financing.

8) The EAT takes title to the relinquished property.

9) The taxpayer takes title to the replacement property. This completes the Like Kind exchange part of the transaction.

   Critical: The relinquished property must be transferred to the EAT before the replacement property is transferred to the taxpayer.

10) The EAT gets a third party contract to purchase the relinquished property, or if the taxpayer already had a contract on the relinquished property, it is assigned to the EAT.

11) Before the end of the 180 day period the EAT transfers the relinquished property title to the third party buyer.

12) The proceeds from the sale are sent by the EAT to any lenders <u>on the replacement property</u> to

pay down the principal. If the taxpayer purchased the replacement property with cash, then any proceeds would go to the taxpayer. Boot would be avoided because cash-in offsets cash-out.

13) Exchangor reports exchange to IRS on Form 8824. The EAT reports the transaction to the IRS and State tax authorities.

6. MODIFICATION TO REVENUE PROCEDURE 2000-37.
IRS Revenue Procedure 2004-51 modified Revenue Procedure 2000-37 by adding paragraph .05 Limitation, as follows to Section 4.

> **.05 Limitation**. This revenue procedure does not apply to replacement property held in a QEAA if the property is owned by the taxpayer within the 180 day period ending on the date of transfer of qualified indicia of ownership of the property to an exchange accommodation titleholder.

This limitation is in effect for transfers of ownership to an EAT after July 19, 2004.

7. SAFE HARBOR vs. FRIENDLY THIRD PARTY ARRANGEMENTS.
While the Revenue Procedure establishes specific "safe harbor" procedures, it permits continued use of currently used parking or friendly third party arrangements. The three most important differences are: (a) the need for a written Qualified Exchange Accommodation Agreement; (b) the restriction on the use of a disqualified person as the exchange accommodation titleholder; and (c) the 180 day limit which starts when the eventual replacement property is transferred to the exchange accommodation titleholder.

> **Important:** When improvements are to be built on the replacement property, the 180 day limit may severely limit the use of the option to use the "safe harbor" procedures.

8. FRIENDLY THIRD PARTY HOLDER – NON SAFE HARBOR.
When the time period for the eventual acquisition of the replacement property by the exchangor would exceed the 180 day restriction of ownership by the exchange accommodation titleholder, then a "friendly third party" must purchase the replacement property and "own and operate it" until the exchangor is ready to take title.

The most important factor, when a third party such as a friend or in-law, the builder or a separate entity purchases the exchangor's eventual replacement property, is that the third party not be considered by the IRS **to be an agent of the exchangor**.

A recent IRS action gives some guidance as to what should be done to avoid the third party being considered an agent. Specifically in Private Letter Ruling 2001-11025, December 8, 2000, the IRS indicated three general requirements must be present in a non-safe harbor reverse exchange setting.

> **First**, the taxpayer/ exchangor must demonstrate its intent to achieve an exchange and the properties to be exchanged must be like kind and for a qualified use.
>
> **Second**, the steps in the various transfers must be part of an integrated plan to exchange the relinquished property for the replacement property; and
>
> **Third**, the party holding the replacement property **must not be the taxpayer's agent**.

To satisfy the above requirements the following is a list of actions to be considered:

a. There is a current Exchange and Escrow Account Agreement in place between the taxpayer/ exchangor and the Qualified Intermediary.

b. If the taxpayer has the replacement property under contract, it is assigned to the third party.

c. The third party must be acting for its own business and account in all transactions. The third party should have the risk of loss or condemnation.

d. The third party has risk and an equity position in the replacement property. The third party should have the benefits and burdens of ownership.

e. The third party must be the owner of the replacement property. It must be in title. A limited liability corporation (LLC) may be established as the third party.

f. Any agreement does not use a "put", that is, the right of the third party to transfer the property back to the taxpayer or other third party.

g. The third party should not be a related or a disqualified party.

h. The exchangor's purchase price for the replacement property should

increase over time to provide for a return on the invested equity of the third party.

i. That the third party be responsible (full recourse) on all loans for it to purchase the replacement property. While the taxpayer may guarantee the loan, interest payments should be made by the third party.

j. That any down payment on the replacement property come from the third party's account and not directly from the taxpayer. The taxpayer may loan funds to the third party.

k. The taxpayer should not authorize the third party to enter into contracts on its behalf.

l. Money must pass properly between the taxpayer and the third party, such as with any lease payments.

m. If the property is to be leased to the taxpayer by the third party, a fair market rent should be charged, and any landlord tenant relationship must be formally established and executed.

n. The third party must report its income and expenses on its own federal and state tax returns.

o. That any contract for construction on the replacement property must be between the third party and the contractor.

9. TO-BE-BUILT EXCHANGES. In addition to the reverse situation above a situation can occur when a taxpayer/exchangor desires that a house or other improvement be built on their replacement property. The most common situation is when the taxpayer has a contract on the property they are selling (the property to be relinquished) and wish to purchase a replacement property lot and have a house built on it. Often a taxpayer will plan to take title to the replacement property lot, and then contract to have a house built on the lot. <u>If the taxpayer takes title to the lot, the exchange is completed and any additional improvements are not like-kind.</u>

In most cases, the purchase price for the lot will not satisfy the reinvestment requirements for the exchange. (If the price of the lot is equal to or greater than the adjusted sale price of the relinquished property, then only the lot is purchased and the exchange is completed.)

Thus, a builder or a non-related third party must purchase the lot , take title and start construction. If the taxpayer already has a contract on a replacement property lot, it must be assigned to the third party or the builder. The taxpayer may lend the funds or guarantee the loan of the third party or builder to purchase the property and start construction.

As outlined above the third party or builder must not be an agent of the taxpayer. The third party or builder should have economic risk at stake in the purchase of the land and building of the improvements.

Then the taxpayer has a real estate purchase contract prepared which provides for the taxpayer to purchase from the third party or builder the replacement property lot with a house built thereon to their specifications. The contract should provide for transfer of the property before the end of the 180 day exchange period. The contract may also provide for the payment of additional deposits as construction progress is made.

After the relinquished property goes to settlement, the Qualified Intermediary will be holding exchange escrow funds which may be used toward the purchase of the replacement property. Once the real estate purchase contract for the replacement property is assigned to the Qualified Intermediary, the exchange escrow funds may be disbursed by the Qualified Intermediary in accordance with the contract.

In a to-be-built exchange within 45 days of the transfer of the relinquished property the taxpayer/exchangor must provide an identification to the Qualified Intermediary, in writing and signed, which provides the <u>legal description</u> for the replacement property and "<u>as much detail regarding construction of the improvements as is practicable</u>". The regulation is unclear as to the detail required, but a prudent taxpayer would provide as much detail as they can.

The exchangor must receive the replacement property within the 180 day exchange period. The replacement property received must be "substantially" the same property as identified. For real property, if the construction is not complete by the 180th day, the property must be transferred to the exchangor. The property received will be considered to be substantially the same property as identified only if, had production been completed, it would have been considered as substantially the same property as identified. The exchange value transferred should be adjusted by the value of the work not completed.

10. TAXPAYER OWNS REPLACEMENT PROPERTY LOT. On occasion the situation will occur where the taxpayer already owns the lot on which they desire to build the replacement property. As stated above — an improvement put on property already owned is not like kind.

The taxpayer basically has two options — to sell the property in a taxable sale to the builder or a third party, OR to lease the land to the contractor or third party for a term in excess of 30 years plus the time required to complete the construction of the desired improvements. A lease of real estate for over thirty years, including options, is considered real property and thus qualifies as a replacement property.

The contractor or third party constructs the improvements on the leasehold, and then conveys the lessee's interest in the ground lease and the ownership of the improvements to the taxpayer as replacement property. There must be at least 30 years remaining on the lease when it is conveyed back to the taxpayer.

> **Caution:** In IRS Revenue Procedure 2004-51 the IRS stated they were opposed to and were studying "transactions in which a person related to the taxpayer (which includes the taxpayer) transfers a leasehold interest in land to an accommodation party (like a builder) and the accommodation party makes improvements to the land and transfers the leasehold with the improvements to the taxpayer in exchange for other real estate".

Notes

REPORTING THE EXCHANGE

1. WHEN DO WE REPORT THE EXCHANGE TO THE IRS? The exchange is reported to the IRS for the tax year in which the first relinquished property is transferred. Regardless of the fact that the replacement property(ies) are transferred in the following tax year.

Example: Exchangor settles on relinquished property on Dec. 15, 2004 — and then settles on replacement property May 1, 2005.

Exchangor would file Form 8824 with 2004 return, after filing an **on time** request for an extension.

2. HOW DO WE REPORT THE EXCHANGE? The Exchange is reported on IRS Form 8824, Like-Kind Exchanges. The Form 8824 is divided into three parts:

Part I. Information on the Like-Kind Exchange.
Part II. Related Party Exchange Information, and
Part III. Realized Gain or (Loss), Recognized Gain, and Basis of Like-Kind Property Received

If the exchangor has recognized gain, in addition to Form 8824, the exchangor may need to report the gain on IRS Form 4797, 'Sales of Business Property', Schedule D (Form 1040), 'Capital Gains and Losses', and/or Form 6252, 'Installment Sale Income'. See paragraph 6 below.

3. COMPLETING PART I — INFORMATION ON THE LIKE-KIND EXCHANGE. For lines 1 and 2 in Part I the exchangor should show for real property the address, and type of property. For personal property a short description should be entered. All property involved in each exchange is included on the single Form 8824. Include an attachment if additional space is required. Line 5 is normally the date the qualified intermediary was provided the identification of the replacement property. In the event the replacement property is settled prior to the 45th day, then separate identification is not required, and the transfer date for the replacement property may be shown on Line 5.

If you made more then one like-kind exchange in the same year - (a) you may report each exchange on a separate Form 8824, or (b) you may file only one summary Form 8824 and attach your own statement showing all the information requested on Form 8824 for each exchange. Include your name and tax ID number at the top of each page of the statement. On the summary Form 8824, enter only your name and tax ID number, then the word "Summary" on Line 1, the total **recognized** gain from all exchanges on Line 23, and the total basis of all like-kind property received on Line 25.

4. COMPLETING PART II — RELATED PARTY EXCHANGE INFORMATION. Part II is only completed when either the relinquished property was transferred to a related party and/or the replacement property was purchased from a related party, directly or indirectly. A related party includes the exchangor's spouse, child, grandchild, parent, grand parent, brother or sister, or a related corporation, S corporation, partnership, or trust in which the exchangor has over a 50% interest. See IRC Section 1031(f). If the exchange is made with a related party then you must also file Form 8824 for the 2 years following the year of exchange. See specific IRS Instructions for Line 7.

5. COMPLETING PART III — REALIZED AND RECOGNIZED GAIN, and BASIS OF NEW PROPERTY. Part III is the most important and most difficult part of the form to complete. Part III provides for the reporting of:

a. Ordinary gain (or loss) on 'other property' (i.e. non-like property) given up (see lines 12, 13, and 14)

b. Ordinary income under the recapture rules (see lines 21 and 22, and Instructions). Do not confuse with recapture of Section 1250 depreciation. There is no recapture if depreciable real property is exchanged for other depreciable real property. If depreciable real property is exchanged for non-depreciable real property (ex: rental house for land) then the total depreciation taken in excess of straight line could be recaptured. If the value of depreciable property received in the exchange (ex: improvements to the land) exceeds the amount of additional or excess depreciation, then no depreciation will be recaptured. Few properties exist today that have excess depreciation.

c. Multi-Asset Exchanges. Note that Multi-Asset exchanges are covered in detail in Section 1.1031(j)-1 of the regulations. An exchange is only reported as a multi-asset exchange if the exchangor transferred **AND** received more than one group of like-kind properties, or cash or other non-like property. Few real estate exchanges are multi-asset exchanges.

d. Realized Gain, Recognized Gain and Basis of Like-Kind Property Received. This is the primary purpose of Part III and Form 8824. **To complete Part III starting on Line 15 requires the use of the Worksheet enclosed**.

> **EXAMPLE:** To show the use of the Worksheet we will use the following example of an exchange transaction. In this example the exchangor will **buy up in value and reinvest all the cash proceeds received**. This situation best demonstrates the vast majority of completed exchanges.
>
> 1. *Basis.* The cost basis in the property being relinquished (with improvements) is $150,000, and $45,000 has been taken in depreciation over a ten year period.
>
> 2. *Relinquished Property.* The relinquished property contract price is $500,000 and the current debt to be paid off at settlement is $90,000.
>
> The exchangor had $40,000 in exchange expenses and the $370,000 in proceeds (exchange escrow funds) were placed in a qualified escrow account by the Qualified Intermediary.
>
> 3. *Replacement Property.* The replacement property was purchased for $550,000 and a new loan was obtained for $250,000. The cash down payment was $370,000 and exchange expenses were $5,000.

The Worksheet is broken down into four steps as follows:

STEP 1   IT IS IMPORTANT TO READ EACH NOTE !!

Gain Realized from Property Relinquished. The first step is to determine the amount of total capital gain that is being realized.

1. FMV of Relinquished Property (Note 1)		$500,000
Note 1: FMV is normally contract price		
2. Less: Adjusted Basis		
2a. Cost (with improvements)	$150,000	
2b. Less: Depreciation	– 45,000	–105,000
3. Less: Total Exchange Expenses (Note 2)		

Note 2: Exchange expenses include allowable
selling expenses for the relinquished property
and the acquisition cost of replacement properties.

3a. Relinquished Property	$40,000	
3b. Replacement Property	+5,000	-45,000
4. Equals Realized Gain		$350,000

Line 4 is posted to Line 19 on Form 8824

STEP 2

Determining Recognized Gain. This is the most important step in the process as it establishes how much of the Capital Gain realized will in fact be recognized and become taxable income. Line 15 at the end of Step 2 reflects the taxable Boot and is transferred to Line 15 on Form 8824 — **"the boot line"**

5. Relief of Debt on relinquished property $ 90,000

6. Less: Debt acquired on replacement property   – 250,000

7. Equals Net relief of Liabilities [Not less then 0]   -0-

These 3 lines determine if there is any mortgage boot.
If debt acquired is less then debt relief mortgage boot results.
Answer may not be less then zero because excess mortgage
cannot offset cash boot.

WORKSHEET TO COMPLETE
Part III of IRS LIKE-KIND EXCHANGE FORM 8824
(Bold line numbers on the right refer to Form 8824)

			Line On
STEP 1. Gain Realized from Property Relinquished—			**Form 8824**

STEP 1. Gain Realized from Property Relinquished—

			Line On Form 8824
1. FMV of Relinquished Property (Note 1)			$ 500,000
2. less: Adjusted Basis			
2a. Cost (with improvements)	$ 150,000		
2b. less: Depreciation Allowed	– 45,000	– 105,000	
3. less: Total Exchange Expenses (Note 2)			
3a. Relinquished Property	$ 40,000		
3b. Replacement Property	+ 5,000	– 45,000	
4. Equals **Realized Gain**		$ 350,000	**(Line 19)**

STEP 2. Recognized Gain—

5. Relief of debt on relinquished property	$ 90,000	
6. less: Debt acquired on replacement property	– 250,000	
7. Equals Net relief of liabilities (Not less then 0)	$ 0	
8. plus: Cash (Down Payment) received (Note 3)	+ 410,000	
9. less: Cash paid (Down payment) (Note 4)	– 370,000	
10. less: Total Exchange Expenses - (from Line 3)	– 45,000	
11. less: FMV of 'other property' relinquished	– 0	
12. Equals total Boot received (Not less then 0)	– 0	
13. plus: FMV of 'other property', cash & Notes received	+ 0	
14. Equals total NET boot received (Lines 12 + 13)	$ 0	
15. **Recognized Gain** (Taxable income)		
(the smaller of Line 4 or 14 above)	$ 0	**(Line 15)**

STEP 3. Realized Gain Deferred

16. Realized Gain (Line 4)	$ 350,000	
17. less: Recognized Gain (taxable income - Line 15 above)	0	
18. Equals **Realized Gain Deferred**	$ 350,000	**(Line 24)**

STEP 4. Basis of New Property

19. FMV of Replacement Property (Note 1)	$ 500,000	**(Line 16)**
20. less: Realized Gain Deferred (Line 18 above)	– 350,000	
21. Equals **Total Basis is New Property(ies)**	$ 200,000	
		(Lines 25 & 18)

NOTES:

    (1) FMV is normally contract price.

    (2) Exchange expenses are allowable selling expenses for the relinquished property and the acquisition cost of replacement properties.

    (3) FMV of relinquished property (Line 1) less debt relief (Line 5) less FMV of 'other property' received, including value of owner held Notes (Line 13) should equal cash received.

    (4) Cash down payment is normally the difference between contract price and loan amount, less any seller non-closing cost credits/allowances.ws:

STEP 1

IT IS IMPORTANT TO READ EACH NOTE !!

Gain Realized from Property Relinquished. The first step is to determine the amount of total capital gain that is being realized.

1. FMV of Relinquished Property (Note 1)		$500,000
Note 1: FMV is normally contract price		
2. Less: Adjusted Basis		
2a. Cost (with improvements)	$150,000	
2b. Less: Depreciation	– 45,000	– 105,000
3. Less: Total Exchange Expenses (Note 2)		
Note 2: Exchange expenses include allowable selling expenses for the relinquished property and the acquisition cost of replacement properties.		
3a. Relinquished Property	$40,000	
3b.Replacement Property	+ 5,000	– 45,000
4. Equals Realized Gain		$350,000

Line 4 is posted to Line 19 on Form 8824

STEP 2

Determining Recognized Gain. This is the most important step in the process as it establishes how much of the Capital Gain realized will in fact be recognized and be-come taxable income. Line 15 at the end of Step 2 reflects the taxable Boot and is transferred to Line 15 on Form 8824 — **"the boot line"**

5. Relief of Debt on relinquished property	$ 90,000
6. Less: Debt acquired on replacement property	– 250,000
7. Equals Net relief of Liabilities [Not less then 0]	-0-
These 3 lines determine if there is any mortgage boot. If debt acquired is less than debt relief mortgage boot results. Answer may not be less than zero because excess mortgage cannot offset cash boot.	
8. Plus: Cash down payment received (Note 3)	+ 410,000
Note 3: FMV of relinquished property (line 1) less debt relief (line 5) less FMV of 'other property received,	

including value of owner held Notes (Line 13) should
equal cash received.

9. Less: Cash paid (down payment) (Note 4)   – 370,000
    Note 4: Cash down payment is normally the difference
    between replacement property contract price and loan
    amount, less any seller non-closing cost credits/allowances

10. Less: Total Exchange Expenses (from Line 3 above)   – 45,000

11. Less: FMV of 'other property' relinquished   -0-
    'Other property' is non-like property, such as personal property

12. Equals total boot received (Not less then 0)   -0-

13. Plus: FMV of 'other property', cash & Notes received   -0-

14. Equals total NET boot received (Lines 12 + 13)   -0-

15. **Recognized Gain** (Taxable Income)
    [the smaller of Line 4 or 14 above]   **$ -0-**

Line 15 is posted to Line 15 on IRS Form 8824

STEP 3

Realized Gain Deferred. This step determines how much of the realized gain will be deferred.

16. Realized Gain (from Line 4 above) $350,000

17. Less: Recognized Gain (Taxable Income)   –   0

18. Equals **Realized Gain deferred** $350,000

Line 18 is posted to Line 24 on IRS Form 8824

Form **8824**	**Like-Kind Exchanges**	OMB No. 1545-1190
Department of the Treasury Internal Revenue Service	(and section 1043 conflict-of-interest sales) ▶ **Attach to your tax return.**	20**04** Attachment Sequence No. **109**

Name(s) shown on tax return	Identifying number

Part I Information on the Like-Kind Exchange

Note: *If the property described on line 1 or line 2 is real or personal property located outside the United States, indicate the country.*

1 Description of like-kind property given up ▶ single family home – 123 Baker Street, Anytown, VA

2 Description of like-kind property received ▶ single family home 456 Beach Road, Anyplave, NC

3 Date like-kind property given up was originally acquired (month, day, year)	**3**	1 / 10 / 95
4 Date you actually transferred your property to other party (month, day, year)	**4**	12 / 20 / 04
5 Date like-kind property you received was identified by written notice to another party (see instructions for 45-day written notice requirement) (month, day, year)	**5**	12 / 30 / 04
6 Date you actually received the like-kind property from other party (month, day, year) (see instructions)	**6**	1 / 20 / 05

7 Was the exchange of the property given up or received made with a related party, either directly or indirectly (such as through an intermediary) (see instructions)? If "Yes," complete Part II. If "No," go to Part III . . . ☐ Yes ☒ No

Part II Related Party Exchange Information

8 Name of related party	Relationship to you	Related party's identifying number
Address (no., street, and apt., room, or suite no., city or town, state, and ZIP code)		

9 During this tax year (and before the date that is 2 years after the last transfer of property that was part of the exchange), did the related party directly or indirectly (such as through an intermediary) sell or dispose of any part of the like-kind property received from you in the exchange? . . . . ☐ Yes ☐ No

10 During this tax year (and before the date that is 2 years after the last transfer of property that was part of the exchange), did you sell or dispose of any part of the like-kind property you received?. . . . . ☐ Yes ☐ No

*If both lines 9 and 10 are "No" and this is the year of the exchange, go to Part III. If both lines 9 and 10 are "No" and this is **not** the year of the exchange, stop here. If either line 9 or line 10 is "Yes," complete Part III and report on this year's tax return the deferred gain or (loss) from line 24 **unless** one of the exceptions on line 11 applies.*

11 If one of the exceptions below applies to the disposition, check the applicable box:

a ☐ The disposition was after the death of either of the related parties.

b ☐ The disposition was an involuntary conversion, and the threat of conversion occurred after the exchange.

c ☐ You can establish to the satisfaction of the IRS that neither the exchange nor the disposition had tax avoidance as its principal purpose. If this box is checked, attach an explanation (see instructions).

Part III Realized Gain or (Loss), Recognized Gain, and Basis of Like-Kind Property Received

Caution: *If you transferred **and** received (a) more than one group of like-kind properties or (b) cash or other (not like-kind) property, see **Reporting of multi-asset exchanges** in the instructions.*

Note: *Complete lines 12 through 14 **only** if you gave up property that was not like-kind. Otherwise, go to line 15.*

12 Fair market value (FMV) of other property given up	**12**	
13 Adjusted basis of other property given up	**13**	
14 Gain or (loss) recognized on other property given up. Subtract line 13 from line 12. Report the gain or (loss) in the same manner as if the exchange had been a sale	**14**	
15 Cash received, FMV of other property received, plus net liabilities assumed by other party, reduced (but not below zero) by any exchange expenses you incurred (see instructions)	**15**	0
16 FMV of like-kind property you received	**16**	550,000
17 Add lines 15 and 16	**17**	550,000
18 Adjusted basis of like-kind property you gave up, net amounts paid to other party, plus any exchange expenses **not** used on line 15 (see instructions)	**18**	200,000
19 **Realized gain or (loss).** Subtract line 18 from line 17	**19**	350,000
20 Enter the smaller of line 15 or line 19, but not less than zero	**20**	0
21 Ordinary income under recapture rules. Enter here and on Form 4797, line 16 (see instructions) .	**21**	0
22 Subtract line 21 from line 20. If zero or less, enter -0-. If more than zero, enter here and on Schedule D or Form 4797, unless the installment method applies (see instructions)	**22**	0
23 **Recognized gain.** Add lines 21 and 22	**23**	0
24 Deferred gain or (loss). Subtract line 23 from line 19. If a related party exchange, see instructions	**24**	350,000
25 **Basis of like-kind property received.** Subtract line 15 from the sum of lines 18 and 23 . .	**25**	200,000

For Paperwork Reduction Act Notice, see page 4. Cat. No. 12311A Form **8824** (2004)

STEP 4

Basis of New Property. This step determines what the basis will be in the new properties. From this basis is subtracted the proportionate value of the land. The balance is the value of the improvements for depreciation purposes. See paragraph 7 below for the revised rules on depreciation of the replacement property.

19. FMV of Replacement Property $550,000
    Line 19 is posted to Line 16 on IRS Form 8824

20. Less: Realized Gain Deferred (from Line 18 above)   –350,000

21. Equals **Total Basis in New Property(ies)** $200,000

    Line 21 is posted to both Lines 18 and 25 on IRS Form 8824

Completion of IRS Form 8824. With the lines posted from the Worksheet the remaining open lines in Part III can then be calculated. (see also IRS Instructions for Form 8824). Visit IRS web site www.irs.gov and search for Form 8824. Select current Form 8824 Fill-in Form. You can type your information in and print out a final copy.

6. **Additional Forms May Be Required.** Once Form 8824 is completed then any additional forms required may be completed. If Line 22, Form 8824 is **zero** – congratulations – no additional forms are required.

    a. Form 4797, 'Sales of Business Property'. Use Form 4797 to report the exchange of property used in your trade or business or held for production of rents. In the unlikely event you have gain on Line 21 on Form 8824 to be recaptured as ordinary income it will be shown on Line 16, Form 4797. From Line 22 on Form 8824, transfer the remaining realized gain (that portion not being reported as an installment sale) to Line 5 on Form 4797. For individual taxpayers this gain will be combined with other gains or losses and posted to Line 11, Schedule D, Form 1040.

    b. Schedule D, Form 1040, 'Capital Gains & Losses'. For investment property not reported on Form 4797 transfer Line 22, Form 8824 (except installment sale amount) directly to Line 11, Schedule D, Form 1040.

    If Line 16, Schedule D shows a gain and you took Section 1250 depreciation then on Line 19, Schedule D enter the amount from Line 18 of the Worksheet on Page D-8 of "Instructions for Schedule D". Section 1250 property is basically all rental real estate on which depreciation is taken.

        Important: Start the Page D-8 Worksheet by entering on Line 12 the **smaller** of (a) the Section 1250 depreciation taken on the relinquished property (see Step 1, line 2.b. of Worksheet enclosed) **or** (b) the recognized gain from Line 22, Form 8824.

    c. Form 6252, Installment Sale Income. That portion of the amount on Line 22, Form 8824 to be treated as an installment sale is reported on Form 6252. If there is any installment sale income then it is carried forward from Line 26, Form 6252 and reported on Line 11, Schedule D or line 4, Form 4797. (see IRS Publication 537, Installment Sales)

    d. Schedule E and Form 8582, Passive Activity Loss Limitations. If you have suspended passive losses from the rental property you are exchanging then you may use those losses to offset any taxable boot you may be receiving. Use Worksheet 5 to Form 8582 to determine the amount of allowed loss (column c) for the specific property being exchanged. This allowed loss then is posted to Line 23, Schedule E. Any suspended passive losses on the exchanged property not used are carried forward to the replacement property (see IRS Publication 925, Passive Activity and At-Risk Rules, and the Instructions for Form 8582).

7. DEPRECIATION OF REPLACEMENT PROPERTY. In January 2000 IRS Notice 2000-4 described the way a new replacement property was to be depreciated. Then in early 2004 the IRS published in T.D. 9115 detailed temporary and proposed regulations amending Section 168. Under the new regulations the general rule remains that the taxpayer must depreciate the remaining relinquished property adjusted basis (called the exchanged basis) over the remaining recovery period using the same depreciation method as if it were a continuation of the relinquished property depreciation schedule. However, if the replacement property is not residential, then the remaining exchanged basis and the new excess basis would be depreciated using the 39 year schedule.

Any increase in the basis (called the *excess basis*) will be treated as newly acquired property and will be depreciated over 27.5 or 39 years using a new straight line depreciation schedule. No depreciation will be claimed for the period between the transfer of the relinquished property and the receipt of the replacement property.

The new regulation does permit the taxpayer to elect out of the rules and to treat the entire replacement property as a new asset. To make this election see IRS instructions for IRS Form 4562, *Depreciation and Amortization*.

Example: An exchangor has been taking depreciation for 10 years on a residential rental purchased for $150,000. He has taken $4,500 in depreciation annually leaving an exchanged basis of $105,000. If he purchases a residential replacement property with a total new basis of $200,000 (per line 25 of Form 8824) his depreciation schedules for the replacement property would be as follows:

Continuation of Old Schedule for Remaining 17.5 years: $4,500 per year for 17.5 years

New Schedule for Amount of Excess Basis for 27.5 years: If the value of the new property depreciable improvements were 82.5% then the $95,000 increase in basis ($200,000 -105,000) would be depreciated as follows: $95,000 X 82.5% = $78,375 divided by 27.5 years. The result would be $2,850 in annual depreciation to be taken for 27.5 years.

Note: The above applies to real estate replacement property depreciation. The temporary regulations also cover Involuntary Conversions under IRC 1033, and other like-kind exchanges. For complete text see IRB 2004-14, April 5, 2004, T.D. 9115, at www.irs.gov.

Deferred Exchange Allocation Of Settlement Costs

RELINQUISHED PROPERTY

Non-Exchange Expenses

HUD 1 Line #	Item (note 1)	Exchange Expense (note 3)	1040 Schedule E Adjustment/Expense	Debt Relief
700	Commission	X		
800	Loan Fees	X		
1100	Title Charges	X		
1200	Recording Fees	X		
1300	Additional Charges	X		
	Termite	X		
	Courier Fees	X		
	Exchange Fees	X		
406 - 412	Pre-paid by Seller		X	
	HOA/Condo Fee		X	
	Taxes		X	
504 -	Pay-off of Mortgage Principal			X
	Pay-off Interest		X	
	Lender Charges		X	
510 - 519	Items Unpaid by Exchangor			
	Taxes		X	
	HOA/Condo Fees		X	
	Escrow for Repairs	X	X	

REPLACEMENT PROPERTY

Non-Exchange Expenses

HUD 1 Line #	Item	Exchange Expense (note 3)	1040 Schedule E Adjustment/Expense	Loan Costs
700	Commission	X		
800-	Loan Fees			X
801 - 802	Loan Points			X (note 2)
803	Appraisal Fee			X
900	Prepaids		X	
	Interest		X	
	Insurance		X	
100	HOA/Condo Fee		X	
1000	Lender Reserves (Taxes + Insurance)		X (note 4)	
1100	Title Charges	X		
	Title Insurance	X		
1200	Recording Fees	X		
1300	Additional Charges	X		
	Exchange Fees	X		
	Termite	X		
	Courier Fees	X		
	Survey	X		

Notes: (1) Include items paid outside of closing (POC), (2) Points paid for loan are amortized over the life of the loan, (3) Exchange expense relates to the costs to dispose of relinquished property and costs to acquire replacement property, (4) Deductible when paid by lender.

WORKSHEET TO COMPLETE
Part III of IRS LIKE-KIND EXCHANGE FORM 8824
(Bold line numbers on the right refer to Form 8824)

Line On
Form 8824

STEP 1. Gain Realized from Property Relinquished —

1. FMV of Relinquished Property (Note 1) $ _____
2. less: Adjusted Basis
   2a. Cost (with improvements) $ _____
   2b. less: Depreciation Allowed   – _____   – _____
3. less: Total Exchange Expenses (Note 2)
   3a. Relinquished Property $ _____
   3b. Replacement Property   + _____   – _____
4. Equals **Realized Gain** $ _____   **(Line 19)**

STEP 2. Recognized Gain —

5. Relief of debt on relinquished property $ _____
6. less: Debt acquired on replacement property   – _____
7. Equals Net relief of liabilities (Not less then 0) $ _____
8. plus: Cash (Down Payment) received (Note 3)   + _____
9. less: Cash paid (Down payment) (Note 4)   – _____
10. less: Total Exchange Expenses - (from Line 3)   – _____
11. less: FMV of 'other property' relinquished   – _____
12. Equals total Boot received (Not less then 0) $ _____
13. plus: FMV of 'other property', cash & Notes received   + _____
14. Equals total NET boot received (Lines 12 + 13) $ _____
15. **Recognized Gain** (Taxable income)
(the smaller of Line 4 or 14 above) $ _____   **(Line 15)**

STEP 3. Realized Gain Deferred

16. Realized Gain (Line 4) $ _____
17. less: Recognized Gain (taxable income - Line 15 above)   – _____
18. Equals **Realized Gain Deferred** $ _____   **(Line 24)**

STEP 4. Basis of New Property

19. FMV of Replacement Property (Note 1) $ _____   **(Line 16)**
20. less: Realized Gain Deferred (Line 18 above)   – _____
21. Equals **Total Basis is New Property(ies)** $ _____

(Lines 25 & 18)

NOTES:

(1) FMV is normally contract price.

(2) Exchange expenses are allowable selling expenses for the relinquished property and the acquisition cost of replacement properties. For the replacement property do not include loan costs or prepaids as exhange expenses.

(3) FMV of relinquished property (Line 1) less debt relief (Line 5) less FMV of 'other property' received, including value of owner held Notes (Line 13) should equal cash received.

(4) Cash down payment is normally the difference between contract price and loan amount, less any seller non-closing cost credits/allowances.

© 2005, Ed Horan, CES®, Haymarket, VA   e-mail: ed@1031.us

Form **8824**	**Like-Kind Exchanges**	OMB No. 1545-1190
Department of the Treasury Internal Revenue Service	**(and section 1043 conflict-of-interest sales)** ▶ **Attach to your tax return.**	20**04** Attachment Sequence No. **109**

Name(s) shown on tax return	Identifying number

Part I **Information on the Like-Kind Exchange**

Note: *If the property described on line 1 or line 2 is real or personal property located outside the United States, indicate the country.*

1 Description of like-kind property given up ▶ ....

2 Description of like-kind property received ▶ ....

3	Date like-kind property given up was originally acquired (month, day, year)	**3** / /
4	Date you actually transferred your property to other party (month, day, year)	**4** / /
5	Date like-kind property you received was identified by written notice to another party (see instructions for 45-day written notice requirement) (month, day, year)	**5** / /
6	Date you actually received the like-kind property from other party (month, day, year) (see instructions)	**6** / /
7	Was the exchange of the property given up or received made with a related party, either directly or indirectly (such as through an intermediary) (see instructions)? If "Yes," complete Part II. If "No," go to Part III . . . ☐Yes ☐No	

Part II **Related Party Exchange Information**

8 Name of related party	Relationship to you	Related party's identifying number

Address (no., street, and apt., room, or suite no., city or town, state, and ZIP code)

9 During this tax year (and before the date that is 2 years after the last transfer of property that was part of the exchange), did the related party directly or indirectly (such as through an intermediary) sell or dispose of any part of the like-kind property received from you in the exchange? . . . . ☐Yes ☐No

10 During this tax year (and before the date that is 2 years after the last transfer of property that was part of the exchange), did you sell or dispose of any part of the like-kind property you received?. . . . . ☐Yes ☐No

*If both lines 9 and 10 are "No" and this is the year of the exchange, go to Part III. If both lines 9 and 10 are "No" and this is **not** the year of the exchange, stop here. If either line 9 or line 10 is "Yes," complete Part III and report on this year's tax return the deferred gain or (loss) from line 24 **unless** one of the exceptions on line 11 applies.*

11 If one of the exceptions below applies to the disposition, check the applicable box:

a ☐ The disposition was after the death of either of the related parties.

b ☐ The disposition was an involuntary conversion, and the threat of conversion occurred after the exchange.

c ☐ You can establish to the satisfaction of the IRS that neither the exchange nor the disposition had tax avoidance as its principal purpose. If this box is checked, attach an explanation (see instructions).

Part III **Realized Gain or (Loss), Recognized Gain, and Basis of Like-Kind Property Received**

Caution: *If you transferred **and** received (a) more than one group of like-kind properties or (b) cash or other (not like-kind) property, see **Reporting of multi-asset exchanges** in the instructions.*

Note: *Complete lines 12 through 14 **only** if you gave up property that was not like-kind. Otherwise, go to line 15.*

12	Fair market value (FMV) of other property given up	**12**
13	Adjusted basis of other property given up	**13**
14	Gain or (loss) recognized on other property given up. Subtract line 13 from line 12. Report the gain or (loss) in the same manner as if the exchange had been a sale	**14**
15	Cash received, FMV of other property received, plus net liabilities assumed by other party, reduced (but not below zero) by any exchange expenses you incurred (see instructions)	**15**
16	FMV of like-kind property you received	**16**
17	Add lines 15 and 16.	**17**
18	Adjusted basis of like-kind property you gave up, net amounts paid to other party, plus any exchange expenses **not** used on line 15 (see instructions)	**18**
19	**Realized gain or (loss).** Subtract line 18 from line 17	**19**
20	Enter the smaller of line 15 or line 19, but not less than zero	**20**
21	Ordinary income under recapture rules. Enter here and on Form 4797, line 16 (see instructions) .	**21**
22	Subtract line 21 from line 20. If zero or less, enter -0-. If more than zero, enter here and on Schedule D or Form 4797, unless the installment method applies (see instructions)	**22**
23	**Recognized gain.** Add lines 21 and 22	**23**
24	Deferred gain or (loss). Subtract line 23 from line 19. If a related party exchange, see instructions	**24**
25	**Basis of like-kind property received.** Subtract line 15 from the sum of lines 18 and 23 . .	**25**

For Paperwork Reduction Act Notice, see page 4.   Cat. No. 12311A   Form **8824** (2004)

Form 8824 (2004)   Page **2**

Name(s) shown on tax return. Do not enter name and social security number if shown on other side. | Your social security number

| **Part IV** | **Deferral of Gain From Section 1043 Conflict-of-Interest Sales** |

Note: *This part is to be used **only** by officers or employees of the executive branch of the Federal Government for reporting nonrecognition of gain under section 1043 on the sale of property to comply with the conflict-of-interest requirements. This part can be used **only** if the cost of the replacement property exceeds the basis of the divested property.*

26 Enter the number from the upper right corner of your certificate of divestiture. (**Do not** attach a copy of your certificate. Keep the certificate with your records.). ▶ _____ – _____

27 Description of divested property ▶ ....

28 Description of replacement property ▶ ....

29 Date divested property was sold (month, day, year) . . . . | **29** | / /

30 Sales price of divested property (see instructions) . . . . . . | **30** |

31 Basis of divested property . . . . | **31** |

32 **Realized gain.** Subtract line 31 from line 30 . . . . | **32** |

33 Cost of replacement property purchased within 60 days after date of sale . . . . | **33** |

34 Subtract line 33 from line 30. If zero or less, enter -0- . . . . | **34** |

35 Ordinary income under recapture rules. Enter here and on Form 4797, line 10 (see instructions) | **35** |

36 Subtract line 35 from line 34. If zero or less, enter -0-. If more than zero, enter here and on Schedule D or Form 4797 (see instructions) . . . . | **36** |

37 **Deferred gain.** Subtract the sum of lines 35 and 36 from line 32 . . . . | **37** |

38 **Basis of replacement property.** Subtract line 37 from line 33 . . . . | **38** |

General Instructions

Section references are to the Internal Revenue Code unless otherwise noted.

Purpose of Form

Use Parts I, II, and III of Form 8824 to report each exchange of business or investment property for property of a like kind. Certain members of the executive branch of the Federal Government use Part IV to elect to defer gain on conflict-of-interest sales.

Multiple exchanges. If you made more than one like-kind exchange, you may file only a summary Form 8824 and attach your own statement showing all the information requested on Form 8824 for each exchange. Include your name and identifying number at the top of each page of the statement. On the summary Form 8824, enter only your name and identifying number, "Summary" on line 1, the total recognized gain from all exchanges on line 23, and the total basis of all like-kind property received on line 25.

When To File

If during the current tax year you transferred property to another party in a like-kind exchange, you must file Form 8824 with your tax return for that year. Also file Form 8824

for the 2 years following the year of a related party exchange (see the instructions for line 7 on page 3).

Like-Kind Exchanges

Generally, if you exchange business or investment property solely for business or investment property of a like kind, no gain or loss is recognized under section 1031. If, as part of the exchange, you also receive other (not like-kind) property or money, gain is recognized to the extent of the other property and money received, but a loss is not recognized.

Section 1031 does not apply to exchanges of inventory, stocks, bonds, notes, other securities or evidence of indebtedness, or certain other assets. See section 1031(a)(2). In addition, section 1031 does not apply to certain exchanges involving tax-exempt use property subject to a lease. See section 470(e)(4).

Like-kind property. Properties are of like kind if they are of the same nature or character, even if they differ in grade or quality. Personal properties of a like class are like-kind properties. However, livestock of different sexes are not like-kind properties. Also, personal property used predominantly in the United States and personal property used predominantly outside the United States are

not like-kind properties. See Pub. 544, Sales and Other Dispositions of Assets, for more details.

Real properties generally are of like kind, regardless of whether they are improved or unimproved. However, real property in the United States and real property outside the United States are not like-kind properties.

Deferred exchanges. A deferred exchange occurs when the property received in the exchange is received after the transfer of the property given up. For a deferred exchange to qualify as like-kind, you must comply with the 45-day written notice and receipt requirements explained in the instructions for lines 5 and 6.

Multi-asset exchanges. A multi-asset exchange involves the transfer and receipt of more than one group of like-kind properties. For example, an exchange of land, vehicles, and cash for land and vehicles is a multi-asset exchange. An exchange of land, vehicles, and cash for land only is not a multi-asset exchange. The transfer or receipt of multiple properties within one like-kind group is also a multi-asset exchange. Special rules apply when figuring the amount of gain recognized and your basis in properties received in a multi-asset exchange. For details, see Regulations section 1.1031(j)-1.

Form **8824** (2004)

Reporting of multi-asset exchanges. If you transferred and received (a) more than one group of like-kind properties or (b) cash or other (not like-kind) property, do not complete lines 12 through 18 of Form 8824. Instead, attach your own statement showing how you figured the realized and recognized gain, and enter the correct amount on lines 19 through 25. Report any recognized gains on Schedule D; Form 4797, Sales of Business Property; or Form 6252, Installment Sale Income, whichever applies.

Exchanges using a qualified exchange accommodation arrangement (QEAA). If property is transferred to an exchange accommodation titleholder (EAT) and held in a QEAA, the EAT may be treated as the beneficial owner of the property, the property transferred from the EAT to you may be treated as property you received in an exchange, and the property you transferred to the EAT may be treated as property you gave up in an exchange. This may be true even if the property you are to receive is transferred to the EAT before you transfer the property you are giving up. However, the property transferred to you may not be treated as property received in an exchange if you previously owned it within 180 days of its transfer to the EAT. For details, see Rev. Proc. 2000-37 as modified by Rev. Proc. 2004-51. Rev. Proc. 2000-37 is on page 308 of Internal Revenue Bulletin 2000-40 at *www.irs.gov/pub/irs-irbs/irb00-40.pdf.* Rev. Proc. 2004-51 is on page 294 of Internal Revenue Bulletin 2004-33 at *www.irs.gov/irb/2004-33_IRB/ar13.html.*

Additional information. For more information on like-kind exchanges, see section 1031 and its regulations and Pub. 544.

Specific Instructions

Lines 1 and 2. For real property, enter the address and type of property. For personal property, enter a short description. For property located outside the United States, include the country.

Line 5. Enter on line 5 the date of the written notice that identifies the like-kind property you received in a deferred exchange. To comply with the **45-day written notice requirement,** the following conditions must be met.

1. The like-kind property you receive in a deferred exchange must be designated in writing as replacement property either in a document you signed or in a written agreement signed by all parties to the exchange.

2. The document or agreement must describe the replacement property in a clear and recognizable manner. Real property should be described using a legal description, street address, or distinguishable name (for example, "Mayfair Apartment Building").

3. No later than 45 days after the date you transferred the property you gave up:

a. You must send, fax, or hand deliver the document you signed to the person required to transfer the replacement property to you (including a disqualified person) or to another person involved in the exchange (other than a disqualified person), or

b. All parties to the exchange must sign the written agreement designating the replacement property.

Generally, a disqualified person is either your agent at the time of the transaction or a person related to you. For more details, see Regulations section 1.1031(k)-1(k).

Note. If you received the replacement property before the end of the 45-day period, you automatically are treated as having met the 45-day written notice requirement. In this case, enter on line 5 the date you received the replacement property.

Line 6. Enter on line 6 the date you received the like-kind property from the other party. The property must be received by the earlier of the following dates.

● The 180th day after the date you transferred the property given up in the exchange.

● The due date (including extensions) of your tax return for the year in which you transferred the property given up.

Line 7. Special rules apply to like-kind exchanges made with related parties, either directly or indirectly. A **related party** includes your spouse, child, grandchild, parent, grandparent, brother, sister, or a related corporation, S corporation, partnership, trust, or estate. See section 1031(f).

An exchange made **indirectly** with a related party includes:

● An exchange made with a related party through an intermediary (such as a qualified intermediary or an exchange accommodation titleholder, as defined in Pub. 544), or

● An exchange made by a disregarded entity (such as a single member limited liability company) if you or a related party owned that entity.

If the related party (either directly or indirectly) or you dispose of the property received in an exchange before the date that is 2 years after the last transfer of property from the exchange, the deferred gain or (loss) from line 24 must be reported on your return for the year of disposition (unless an exception on line 11 applies).

If you are filing this form for 1 of the 2 years following the year of the exchange, complete Parts I and II. If both lines 9 and 10 are "No," **stop.**

If either line 9 or line 10 is "Yes," and an exception on line 11 applies, check the applicable box on line 11, attach any required explanation, and **stop.** If no line 11 exceptions apply, complete Part III. Report the deferred gain or (loss) from line 24 on this year's tax return as if the exchange had been a sale.

An exchange structured to avoid the related party rules is not a like-kind exchange and may not be reported on Form 8824. Instead, you should report the disposition of the property given up as if the exchange had been a sale. See section 1031(f)(4). Such an exchange includes the transfer of property you gave up to a qualifed intermediary in exchange for property you received that was formerly owned by a related party if the related party received cash or other (not like-kind) property for the property you received, and you used the qualified intermediary to avoid the application of the related party rules. See Rev. Rul. 2002-83 for more details. You can find Rev. Rul. 2002-83 on page 927 of Internal Revenue Bulletin 2002-49 at *www.irs.gov/pub/irs-irbs/irb02-49.pdf.*

Line 11c. If you believe that you can establish to the satisfaction of the IRS that tax avoidance was not a principal purpose of both the exchange and the disposition, attach an explanation. Generally, tax avoidance will not be seen as a principal purpose in the case of:

● A disposition of property in a nonrecognition transaction,

● An exchange in which the related parties derive no tax advantage from the shifting of basis between the exchanged properties, or

● An exchange of undivided interests in different properties that results in each related party holding either the entire interest in a single property or a larger undivided interest in any of the properties.

Lines 12, 13, and 14. If you gave up other property in addition to the like-kind property, enter the fair market value (FMV) and the adjusted basis of the other property on lines 12 and 13, respectively. The gain or (loss) from this property is figured on line 14 and must be reported on your return. Report gain or (loss) as if the exchange were a sale.

Line 15. Include on line 15 the sum of:

● Any cash paid to you by the other party,

● The FMV of other (not like-kind) property you received, if any, and

● Net liabilities assumed by the other party—the excess, if any, of liabilities (including mortgages) assumed by the other party over the total of (a) any liabilities you assumed, (b) cash you paid to the other party, and (c) the FMV of the other (not like-kind) property you gave up.

Reduce the sum of the above amounts (but not below zero) by any exchange expenses you incurred. See the example on page 4.

The following rules apply in determining the amount of liability treated as assumed.

● A recourse liability (or portion thereof) is treated as assumed by the party receiving the property if that party has agreed to and is expected to satisfy the liability (or portion thereof). It does not matter whether the party transferring the property has been relieved of the liability.

● A nonrecourse liability generally is treated as assumed by the party receiving the property subject to the liability. However, if an owner of other assets subject to the same liability agrees with the party receiving the property to, and is expected to, satisfy part or all of the liability, the amount treated as assumed is reduced by the smaller of (a) the amount of the liability that the owner of the other assets has agreed to and is expected to satisfy or (b) the FMV of those other assets.

Line 18. Include on line 18 the sum of:

● The adjusted basis of the like-kind property you gave up,

● Exchange expenses, if any (except for expenses used to reduce the amount reported on line 15), and

● Net amount paid to the other party—the **excess,** if any, of the total of (a) any liabilities you assumed, (b) cash you paid to the other party, and (c) the FMV of the other (not like-kind) property you gave up **over** any liabilities assumed by the other party.

See Regulations section 1.1031(d)-2 and the following example for figuring amounts to enter on lines 15 and 18.

Form 8824 (2004)   Page **4**

Example. A owns an apartment house with an FMV of $220,000, an adjusted basis of $100,000, and subject to a mortgage of $80,000. B owns an apartment house with an FMV of $250,000, an adjusted basis of $175,000, and subject to a mortgage of $150,000.

A transfers his apartment house to B and receives in exchange B's apartment house plus $40,000 cash. A assumes the mortgage on the apartment house received from B, and B assumes the mortgage on the apartment house received from A.

A enters on line 15 only the $40,000 cash received from B. The $80,000 of liabilities assumed by B is not included because it does not exceed the $150,000 of liabilities A assumed. A enters $170,000 on line 18—the $100,000 adjusted basis, plus the $70,000 excess of the liabilities A assumed over the liabilities assumed by B ($150,000 - $80,000).

B enters $30,000 on line 15—the excess of the $150,000 of liabilities assumed by A over the total ($120,000) of the $80,000 of liabilities B assumed and the $40,000 cash B paid. B enters on line 18 only the adjusted basis of $175,000 because the total of the $80,000 of liabilities B assumed and the $40,000 cash B paid does not exceed the $150,000 of liabilities assumed by A.

Line 21. If you disposed of section 1245, 1250, 1252, 1254, or 1255 property (see the instructions for Part III of Form 4797), you may be required to recapture as ordinary income part or all of the realized gain (line 19). Figure the amount to enter on line 21 as follows:

Section 1245 property. Enter the smaller of:

1. The total adjustments for deductions (whether for the same or other property) allowed or allowable to you or any other person for depreciation or amortization (up to the amount of gain shown on line 19), or

2. The gain shown on line 20, if any, plus the FMV of non-section 1245 like-kind property received.

Section 1250 property. Enter the smaller of:

1. The gain you would have had to report as ordinary income because of additional depreciation if you had sold the property (see the Form 4797 instructions for line 26), or

2. The larger of:

a. The gain shown on line 20, if any, or

b. The excess, if any, of the gain in item 1 above over the FMV of the section 1250 property received.

Section 1252, 1254, and 1255 property. The rules for these types of property are similar to those for section 1245 property. See Regulations section 1.1252-2(d) and Temporary Regulations section 16A.1255-2(c) for details. If the installment method applies to this exchange:

1. See section 453(f)(6) to determine the installment sale income taxable for this year and report it on Form 6252.

2. Enter on Form 6252, line 25 or 36, the section 1252, 1254, or 1255 recapture amount you figured on Form 8824, line 21.

Do not enter more than the amount shown on Form 6252, line 24 or 35.

3. Also enter this amount on Form 4797, line 15.

4. If all the ordinary income is not recaptured this year, report in future years on Form 6252 the ordinary income up to the taxable installment sale income, until it is all reported.

Line 22. Report a gain from the exchange of property used in a trade or business (and other noncapital assets) on Form 4797, line 5 or line 16. Report a gain from the exchange of capital assets according to the Schedule D instructions for your return. Be sure to use the date of the exchange as the date for reporting the gain. If the installment method applies to this exchange, see section 453(f)(6) to determine the installment sale income taxable for this year and report it on Form 6252.

Line 24. If line 19 is a loss, enter it on line 24. Otherwise, subtract the amount on line 23 from the amount on line 19 and enter the result. For exchanges with related parties, see the instructions for line 7 on page 3.

Line 25. The amount on line 25 is your basis in the like-kind property you received in the exchange. Your basis in other property received in the exchange, if any, is its FMV.

Section 1043 Conflict-of-Interest Sales (Part IV)

If you sell property at a gain according to a certificate of divestiture issued by the Office of Government Ethics (OGE) and purchase replacement property (permitted property), you may elect to defer part or all of the realized gain. You must recognize gain on the sale only to the extent that the amount realized on the sale exceeds the cost of replacement property purchased within 60 days after the sale. (You also must recognize any ordinary income recapture.) Permitted property is any obligation of the United States or any diversified investment fund approved by the OGE.

 If the property you sold was stock you acquired by exercising a statutory stock option, you may be treated as meeting the holding periods that apply to such stock, regardless of how long you actually held the stock. This may benefit you if you do not defer your entire gain by allowing you to treat the gain as a capital gain instead of ordinary income. You must have sold the stock after October 22, 2004. For details, see section 421(d) or Pub. 525.

Complete Part IV of Form 8824 only if the cost of the replacement property exceeds the basis of the divested property and you elect to defer the gain. Otherwise, report the sale on Schedule D or Form 4797, whichever applies.

Your basis in the replacement property is reduced by the amount of the deferred gain. If you made more than one purchase of replacement property, reduce your basis in the replacement property in the order it was acquired.

Line 30. Enter the amount you received from the sale of the divested property, minus any selling expenses.

Line 35. Follow these steps to determine the amount to enter.

1. Use Part III of Form 4797 as a worksheet to figure ordinary income under the recapture rules.

2. Enter on Form 8824, line 35, the amount from Form 4797, line 31. Do not attach the Form 4797 used as a worksheet to your return.

3. Report the amount from line 35 on Form 4797, line 10, column (g). In column (a), write "From Form 8824, line 35." Do not complete columns (b) through (f).

Line 36. If you sold a capital asset, enter any capital gain from line 36 on Schedule D. If you sold property used in a trade or business (or any other asset for which the gain is treated as ordinary income), report the gain on Form 4797, line 2 or line 10, column (g). In column (a), write "From Form 8824, line 36." Do not complete columns (b) through (f).

Paperwork Reduction Act Notice. We ask for the information on this form to carry out the Internal Revenue laws of the United States. You are required to give us the information. We need it to ensure that you are complying with these laws and to allow us to figure and collect the right amount of tax.

You are not required to provide the information requested on a form that is subject to the Paperwork Reduction Act unless the form displays a valid OMB control number. Books or records relating to a form or its instructions must be retained as long as their contents may become material in the administration of any Internal Revenue law. Generally, tax returns and return information are confidential, as required by section 6103.

The time needed to complete and file this form will vary depending on individual circumstances. The estimated average time is:

Recordkeeping	1 hr., 38 min.
Learning about the law or the form.	27 min.
Preparing the form	59 min.
Copying, assembling, and sending the form to the IRS . .	33 min.

If you have comments concerning the accuracy of these time estimates or suggestions for making this form simpler, we would be happy to hear from you. See the instructions for the tax return with which this form is filed.

Appendices

Appendix A

References

The following publications and sources were used in research and development of this book.

IRS Publication 544, "Sales and Other Dispositions of Assets"

IRS Publication 551, "Basis of Assets"

IRS Publication 527, "Residential Rental Property (Including Rental of Vacation Homes)"

IRS Publication 523, "Selling Your Home"

IRS Instructions for Form 8824, "Like-Kind Exchanges"

IRS Instructions for Form 4797, "Sales of Business Property"

Jeremiah M. Long and Mary Foster, "Tax-Free Exchanges Under §1031", West Group, New York, 2004 with annual update.

Vernon Hoven, "The Real Estate Investor's Tax Guide", Fourth Edition, Dearborn Real Estate Education, Chicago, IL, 2003

Richard A. Robinson, CPA, "Understanding the Tax Part of Real Estate Exchanging", Writers Club Press, NY, 2001

Richard T. Williamson, "Selling Real Estate Without Paying Taxes", Dearborn, Chicago, IL, 2003

Federal Register,Vol 56, No. 84, p.19933, GPO, Washington, D.C. May 1, 1991. (Contains actual text of the tax deferred regulation)

Federal Register,Vol 59, No. 76, p.18747, GPO, Washington, D.C. April 20, 1994. (Contains actual text of the regulation coordinating like-kind exchanges and installment sale rules)

Albert J. Ayella, CPA, "How to Report Like-Kind Exchanges: A Step-by-Step Approach", The Practical Accountant, April 1992, Pages 19-40.

IRS Publications may be obtained by calling 1-800-829-3676 or over the internet at www.irs.gov

REALTY EXCHANGE CORPORATION
"Your nationwide Qualified Intermediary for Tax Deferred Exchanges"
4500 Martinwood Drive, Haymarket, Virginia 20169
1-800-795-0769 (703) 754-9411 Fax: 703-754-0754
www.1031.us

FEE SCHEDULE
(effective January 1, 2001)

1.	Initial Consultation and Contract Addendum	No Charge
2.	Exchange and Escrow Account Agreement and Assignment of Contract (Exchange Agreement is normally signed after ratification of purchase contract on exchange property being relinquished)	No Charge
3.	Exchange Fee (Paid from settlement proceeds of property being relinquished. Includes exchange of a single replacement property.)	$950.00
4.	Exchange Fee for Additional Property (This fee is for each additional replacement or relinquished property which is part of the same exchange.)	$300.00
5.	Administrative fees (such as: Wire transfer fees, Federal Express, Notary, etc.)	At Cost
6.	Rush Service Fee (charged when Realty Exchange Corporation has less then two business days prior to the settlement of relinquished property to complete the exchange documentation)	$200.00

Special Services if requested by Exchangor	
Receipt, transfer and reassignment of Notes	$200.00
Establishment of separate Escrow Account	$200.00

At the completion of the exchange, interest will be paid by Realty Exchange Corporation to the exchangor on the funds held in the Qualified Escrow Account. The interest is paid based on the BB&T Bank Business Money Rate Savings account rate.

Above fees do not include normal settlement and recording fees paid to the Settlement Agent. Also fees for any legal or accounting advice obtained by the exchangor are separate from above fees.

Member of the Federation of Exchange Accommodators
Bonded and Insured

Tax Deferred Exchange Checklist and Documentation Requirements

1. _____ Suggested.   Taxpayer adds Addendum to buyer's offer to show that transaction is a like kind exchange, and to allow contract to be assigned to Qualified Intermediary (QI).

2. _____ **Required.**   A copy of the sales contract is faxed or sent to the QI with the name and phone number of the settlement agent/ attorney.

3. _____ **Required.**   Taxpayer signs QI provided Exchange and Escrow Account Agreement, and Assignment of Contract prior to settlement. Signed documents are returned to QI. §1.1031(k)-1(g)(4)(iii)(B) and (4)(v).

4. _____ **Required.**   Written notification of assignment is provided to all parties of the contract prior to settlement. §1.1031(k)-1(g)(4)(v)

5. _____ **Required.**   Taxpayer keeps QI informed on any changes in closing date or the settlement agent/ attorney.

6. _____ **Required.**   At settlement Qualified Intermediary receives exchange funds and places in qualified escrow account. Taxpayer has no control of funds. §1.1031(k)-1(g)(3)

7. _____ **Required.**   Within 45 days of transfer taxpayer provides signed written notification to QI listing identified replacement properties. §1.1031(k)-1(b)

8. _____ Suggested.   Taxpayer adds to replacement property contract Addendum to show transaction is part of a tax deferred exchange and that exchangor's rights may be assigned.

9. _____ **Required.**   Taxpayer's rights in replacement property contract are assigned to QI prior to settlement. §1.1031(k)-1(g)(4)(v)

10. _____ **Required.**   Written notification of assignment is provided prior to settlement to all parties of the contract. §1.1031(k)-1(g)(4)(v)

11. _____ **Required.**   Within 180 days of transfer of first relinquished property Taxpayer must receive replacement property.§1.1031(k)-1(d)

12. _____ Authorized.   At end of exchange period, QI provides any remaining escrow account funds, and interest earned to Taxpayer. §1.1031(k)-1(h)

13. _____ **Required.**   Exchangor files IRS Form 8824 for tax year in which first relinquished property was transferred. IRS Publication 544.

The Great Real Estate Tax Break
Combining a like kind exchange and the principal residence exclusion

In the Taxpayer Relief Act of 1997 Congress passed a major tax break for everyone who owns their home. When the like kind exchange rules and the homeowner exclusion rules are both used taxpayers can achieve a significant tax break. In October 2004 Congress revised Section 121 to require a principal residence obtained in a like kind exchange to be owned for five years before qualifying for the homeowner exclusion.

Q. What is the principal residence exclusion rule?

A. Married couples filing jointly can exclude up to $500,000 of gain when they sell their principal residence. Single taxpayers can exclude up to $250,000 of their gain. To qualify for the exclusion you must have owned and used the home as a principal residence for an aggregate of two years out of the five years before the sale.

Q. Can I exchange our current rental, investment or business property for a home in a location where we may wish to retire, rent it out, then sell our current principal residence and convert the replacement property to our new principal residence?

A. Yes. This approach will maximize your tax savings. When you transfer your current investment, rental or business property as part of a like kind exchange you defer the tax on the gain. This is reflected in the lower basis assigned to your replacement property. When you sell your current principal residence you exclude the gain. Then after you convert your replacement property to your new principal residence you become eligible once again for exclusion of up to $500,000 of gain after you have owned the replacement property for five years and used it as a principal residence for two years.

Q. When can I convert my investment, rental or business property to personal use?

A. You can convert a rental, investment or business property to personal use at anytime you desire without paying any tax at that time. If you just acquired the property by doing a like kind exchange you must hold the property as an investment, rental or business property. No one can tell you how long the exchange replacement property must be held in that status before you convert it to personal use, but most tax experts recommend not less then one year.

Q. If we do convert our rental to our principal residence how long do we need to own the property before selling it and claiming the exclusion once again ?

A. After converting your rental to your new principal residence you must have owned the property for five years and used it for two years before you can claim the exclusion again. Tax will be due only on any depreciation taken after May 6, 1997. (Prior to passage in October 2004 of H.R. 4520 there was no 5 year ownership restriction.)

Q. Must you buy another property to get the exclusion?

A. No. The previous law (IRC 1034) which required you to purchase another property to "rollover" your gain was abolished in 1997.

Q. Can you combine the principal residence exclusion and like kind exchange on the same property?

A. Yes. If you own a property which part of is your principal residence and part is an investment, rental or business property you may use both the principal residence exclusion and a 1031 like kind exchange. An easy to understand example is the sale of a duplex where you rented out one half and lived in the other half. The gain on the portion in which you lived can be excluded and the tax of the gain on the part you rented out may be deferred using a like kind exchange.

Q. Can the ownership and use tests for the exclusion be met at different times?
A. Yes. You can meet the ownership and use tests during different two year periods. However, you must meet both tests during the five year period ending on the date of the sale.

Q. When you sell the property must you be living there to claim the exclusion?
A. No. You must only have lived in the property for two of the last five years.

Q. Are there any exceptions to the principal residence two year rule?
A. Yes, you may get a reduced exclusion if you must sell due to a job location change that qualifies for the moving expense tax deduction, for health reasons, or under special circumstances.

Q. If you qualify for the exception, how do you figure the reduced exclusion?
A. Take the smaller of - the number of days you lived in the property and the number of days you owned the property during the five years prior to the date of sale. Divide that number by 730 days. Then multiply $250,000 or $500,000 by the decimal you obtained. That amount is your maximum exclusion. (see Worksheet 3 in IRS Publication 523)

Q. How old must you be to claim the exclusion?
A. There is no age restriction. The previous requirement to be 55 or older to get a "once in a life time" exclusion of $125,000 was also abolished in 1997.

Q. Do both married taxpayers have to own the property to exclude up to $500,000 of gain?
A. No. Only one spouse has to own the property. But both must have lived in the property for two years and file a joint return for the year of sale to claim the $500,000 exclusion.

Q. How often can you sell your principal residence and exclude the gain?
A. Once every two years. You cannot exclude the gain on the sale of your principal residence if, during the two year period ending of the date of sale, you sold another principal residence at a gain and excluded all or part of the gain. To exclude up to $500,000 of the gain, neither spouse can have excluded the gain from the sale of a principal residence during the past two years.

Q. If I rented out my principal residence for a while do I have to claim any gain?
A. The gain to be excluded must be reduced by the amount of depreciation taken after May 6, 1997. This recapture of depreciation is then reported on IRS Form Schedule D. (see example in Publication 523)

Q. May the time we were away from our principal residence on vacation still be counted toward the two years we must live in the house to qualify for the exclusion?
A. Yes. Short temporary absences for vacations or other seasonal absences, even if you rent out the property during the absences, are counted as periods of use.

Q. If I use part of my property for business purposes, such as my garage, may I still exclude the gain on that part of the property?
A. If during the past five years that part was used as part of your principal residence for at least two years then you may exclude the gain on that part of the property, except for the depreciation taken.

Q. Where can I get more information?
A. Get a free copy of IRS Publication 523, Selling Your Home, by calling (800)-829-3676, and call us at (800) 795-0769 for a free copy of our information package on How To Do a Tax Deferred Exchange Using a Qualified Intermediary; and contact your tax adviser.

LIKE-KIND PROPERTY EXCHANGE ADDENDUM

Suggest this Addendum be added when contract for the sale of the property to be relinquished is received. The sole purpose of this Addendum is: (1) to show the owner's intent to do a Like-Kind Tax Deferred Exchange in accordance with IRC Regulation Section 1.1031(k)-1, (2) to permit assignment of the relinquished property contract to the Qualified Intermediary, and (3) to advise the purchaser there will be no expense or liability as a result of the exchange.

This addendum is made and entered into on _____ 20 _____ and is an addendum to the Purchase Agreement dated: _____ 20_____,

between: _____ Purchaser

and _____ Owner/Exchangor,

to purchase and exchange the property known as:

_____

_____

Notwithstanding anything in this agreement to the contrary, it is the intent of the Owner/Exchangor to transfer the property to the Purchaser as part of a Like-Kind Tax Deferred Exchange.

It is the intent of the parties that the Owner/Exchangor be allowed to use Section 1031 of the Internal Revenue Code to exchange this property for other replacement property to be identified and acquired later by the Exchangor in accordance with Section 1031 regulations.

This contract may be assigned to Realty Exchange Corporation, as the Qualified Intermediary, solely for the purpose of completing the exchange. The purchaser will be notified in writing when this assignment is made. Title however will be conveyed directly from the Owner/Exchangor to the Purchaser in accordance with Revenue Ruling 90-34.

The Purchaser will be held harmless, and no additional expense or liability will be incurred by the Purchaser as a result of this like-kind exchange. All other items and conditions of this contract remain in full force and effect.

_____
Date

_____
Purchaser

_____
Purchaser

_____
Date

_____
Owner/Exchangor

_____
Owner/Exchangor

Realty Exchange Corporation, Haymarket, VA 1-800-795-0769 Fax: (703) 754-0754

ASSIGNMENT OF CONTRACT

The intent of this assignment of contract is to comply with Section 1.1031(k)-1(g)(4)(iv) and (v) of the Internal Revenue Service Regulations which provides that the contract for the purchase of the Exchangors' relinquished property be assigned to the Qualified Intermediary, and that all parties to the contract notified of the assignment prior to transfer of the property.

****

This assignment of contract is entered into on _____ between _____, Exchangors, and Realty Exchange Corporation, the Qualified Intermediary, with the following terms and conditions:

1. Assignment of Exchange Contract . Exchangors hereby assign to Realty Exchange Corporation all of their rights in the Real Estate Purchase Agreement, as amended, dated _____, by and between: _____, Purchaser(s) and Exchangors, for the exchange and purchase of the property known as:

_____

2. Procedure. Settlement agent will prepare necessary settlement statement to transfer the exchange property from the Exchangors, by and through Realty Exchange Corporation as the Qualified Intermediary, to the Purchaser(s) in accordance with the terms of the Real Estate Purchase Agreement, as amended, and the Exchange Agreement between the Exchangors and Realty Exchange Corporation. The property will be transferred by direct deed from the Exchangors to the Purchaser(s). All costs for the preparation of documentation to transfer subject exchange property, in excess of those agreed to and allocated in the Purchase Agreement, shall be borne by the Exchangors.

3. Liabilities. All of the liabilities, rights, claims and causes of action between the Exchangors and Purchasers shall continue to exist and Exchangors shall not be relieved of same by this assignment. Realty Exchange Corporation shall not be liable to Purchaser for any of Purchaser's damages or claims in the event of any breach by Exchangors; and shall not be responsible for providing any funds or executing any documents which obligates Realty Exchange Corporation to pay any funds except for the disbursement of funds in the any existing exchange escrow. If either the Exchangors or Purchasers name Realty Exchange Corporation in any litigation, that party shall bear all the legal fees of independent counsel retained by Realty Exchange Corporation. All affidavits regarding exchange property relative to property condition, title, mechanics liens, environmental hazards or other matters pertaining to the property shall be obtained by and be the responsibility of the Exchangors. The agreements and warranties herein shall survive closing.

_____
Exchangor

_____
Exchangor

_____
Realty Exchange Corporation
by Cynthia J. Dove, President

REALTY EXCHANGE CORPORATION

"Your Nationwide Qualified Intermediary for Tax Deferred Exchanges"

4500 Martinwood Drive, Haymarket, Virginia 20169   (703) 754-9411

NOTIFICATION of ASSIGNMENT of CONTRACT

_____

To: _____

1. You are hereby notified that _____, Exchangors, assigned all of their rights in the Real Estate Purchase Agreement (Contract), as amended, dated _____, pertaining to _____ _____ to Realty Exchange Corporation, as the Qualified Intermediary.

2. The sole purpose for this assignment is to complete a like-kind exchange as set forth in the Exchange Agreement between the Exchangors and Realty Exchange Corporation. IRS Regulation Section 1.1031 (k)-1 (g)(4)(v) requires you to be notified in writing of this assignment.

3. All of the liabilities, rights, claims and causes of action between the Exchangors and other parties shall continue to exist and Exchangors shall not be relieved of same by this assignment. Realty Exchange Corporation shall not be liable for any damages or claims in the event of any breach by Exchangors; and shall not be responsible for providing any funds or executing any documents which obligates Realty Exchange Corporation to pay any funds. All affidavits regarding exchange property relative to property condition, title, mechanics liens, environmental hazards or other matters pertaining to the property shall be obtained by and be the responsibility of the parties set forth in the contract.

Cynthia J. Dove
President

cc: Exchangors

A. Settlement Statement

U.S. Department of Housing
and Urban Development

OMB No. 2502-0265

B. Type of Loan

1. ☐ FHA 2. ☐ FmHA 3.☐ Conv. Unins.
4. ☐ VA 5. ☐ Conv. Ins.

6. File Number	7. Loan Number	8. Mortgage Insurance Case Number

C. Note: This form is furnished to give you a statement of actual settlement costs. Amounts paid to and by the settlement agent are shown. Items marked "(p.o.c.)" were paid outside the closing; they are shown here for informational purposes and are not included in the totals.

D. Name and Address of Borrower	E. Name and Address of Seller	F. Name and Address of Lender
Donald James Presley William J. Presley Florence I. Presley 26 Brewer Street New London, CT 06320	Gary C. Burfoot, by and through Realty Exchange Corporation 45 Taylor Avenue Norwalk, CT 06354	The Bank of Southeastern Connecticut 716 Broad Street Ext. Waterford, CT 06385

G. Property Location	H. Settlement Agent
27 High Street Mystic, CT 06355	Atty. Kenneth M. McKeever

Place of Settlement
Atty. Kenneth M. McKeever
81 Pennsylvania Avenue
Niantic, CT 06357

I. Settlement Date

J. Summary of Borrower's Transaction		K. Summary of Seller's Transaction	
100. Gross Amount Due From Borrower		**400. Gross Amount Due To Seller**	
101. Contract sales price	137,000.00	401. Contract sales price	137,000.00
102. Personal property		402. Personal property	
103. Settlement charges to borrower (line 1400)	4,809.82	403.	
104.		404.	
105.		405.	
Adjustments for items paid by seller in advance		*Adjustments for items paid by seller in advance*	
106. City/town taxes 10-8 to 12-31-93	459.17	406. City/town taxes 10-8 to 12-31-93	459.17
107. County taxes to		407. County taxes to	
108. Assessments to		408. Assessments to	
109. Sewer use 10-8 to 6-30-94	105.07	409. Sewer use 10-8 to 6-30-94	105.07
110. Fire Dist. 10-8 to 6-30-94	191.52	410. Fire Dist. 10-8 to 6-30-94	191.52
111. Sewer Dist. 10-8 to 12-31-93	31.19	411. Sewer Dist. 10-8 to 12-31-93	31.19
112.		412.	
120. Gross Amount Due From Borrower	142,596.77	**420. Gross Amount Due To Seller**	137,786.95
200. Amounts Paid By Or In Behalf Of Borrower		**500. Reductions In Amount Due To Seller**	
201. Deposit or earnest money	2,000.00	501. Excess deposit (see instructions)	2,000.00
202. Principal amount of new loan(s)	95,900.00	502. Settlement charges to seller (line 1400)	10,566.50
203. Existing loan(s) taken subject to		503. Existing loan(s) taken subject to	
204.		504. Payoff of first mortgage loan CGSB	14,144.00
205.		505. Payoff of second mortgage loan	
206.		506.	
207.		507.	
208.		508.	
209.		509. Exchange escrow funds	111,076.45
Adjustments for items unpaid by seller		*Adjustments for items unpaid by seller*	
210. City/town taxes to		510. City/town taxes to	
211. County taxes to		511. County taxes to	
212. Assessments to		512. Assessments to	
213.		513.	
214.		514.	
215.		515.	
216.		516.	
217.		517.	
218.		518.	
219.		519.	
220. Total Paid By/For Borrower	97,900.00	**520. Total Reduction Amount Due Seller**	137,786.95
300. Cash At Settlement From/To Borrower		**600. Cash At Settlement To/From Seller**	
301. Gross Amount due from borrower (line 120)	142,596.77	601. Gross amount due to seller (line 420)	137,786.95
302. Less amounts paid by/for borrower (line 220)	(97,900.00)	602. Less reductions in amt. due seller (line 520)	(137,786.99)
303. Cash ☒ From ☐ To Borrower	44,696.77	603. Cash ☒ To ☐ From Seller	-0-

SCHEDULE E	**Supplemental Income and Loss**	OMB No. 1545-0074
(Form 1040)	(From rental real estate, royalties, partnerships, S corporations, estates, trusts, REMICs, etc.)	20**04**
Department of the Treasury Internal Revenue Service (99)	▶ **Attach to Form 1040 or Form 1041.** ▶ **See Instructions for Schedule E (Form 1040).**	Attachment Sequence No. **13**

Name(s) shown on return | Your social security number

Part I   Income or Loss From Rental Real Estate and Royalties   **Note.** If you are in the business of renting personal property, use **Schedule C** or **C-EZ** (see page E-3). Report farm rental income or loss from **Form 4835** on page 2, line 40.

1 List the type and location of each **rental real estate property:**

A ....

B ....

C ....

2 For each rental real estate property listed on line 1, did you or your family use it during the tax year for personal purposes for more than the greater of:
- 14 days **or**
- 10% of the total days rented at fair rental value?
(See page E-3.)

	Yes	No
A		
B		
C		

Income:

		Properties A	B	C	Totals (Add columns A, B, and C.)
3 Rents received	3				3
4 Royalties received	4				4

Expenses:

		A	B	C	
5 Advertising	5				
6 Auto and travel (see page E-4)	6				
7 Cleaning and maintenance	7				
8 Commissions	8				
9 Insurance	9				
10 Legal and other professional fees	10				
11 Management fees	11				
12 Mortgage interest paid to banks, etc. (see page E-4)	12				12
13 Other interest	13				
14 Repairs	14				
15 Supplies	15				
16 Taxes	16				
17 Utilities	17				
18 Other (list) ▶	18				
19 Add lines 5 through 18	19				19
20 Depreciation expense or depletion (see page E-4)	20				20
21 Total expenses. Add lines 19 and 20	21				
22 Income or (loss) from rental real estate or royalty properties. Subtract line 21 from line 3 (rents) or line 4 (royalties). If the result is a (loss), see page E-4 to find out if you must file **Form 6198**	22				
23 Deductible rental real estate loss. **Caution.** Your rental real estate loss on line 22 may be limited. See page E-4 to find out if you must file **Form 8582.** Real estate professionals must complete line 43 on page 2	23	( )	( )	( )	( )

24	**Income.** Add positive amounts shown on line 22. **Do not** include any losses	24	
25	**Losses.** Add royalty losses from line 22 and rental real estate losses from line 23. Enter total losses here	25	( )
26	**Total rental real estate and royalty income or (loss).** Combine lines 24 and 25. Enter the result here. If Parts II, III, IV, and line 40 on page 2 do not apply to you, also enter this amount on Form 1040, line 17. Otherwise, include this amount in the total on line 41 on page 2	26	

For Paperwork Reduction Act Notice, see Form 1040 instructions.   Cat. No. 11344L   **Schedule E (Form 1040) 2004**

The Great Homeowners Tax Break
A full explanation of the tax exclusion on the sale of a principal residence

If you currently own a home or plan to purchase one you will be overjoyed to learn about the great tax break Uncle Sam has especially for you as a homeowner. When you sell your principal residence the capital gain on the sale, up to $250,000 or $500,000, will be excluded from your income if you meet the use and ownership tests.

USE TEST

As the taxpayer you have lived in the property for at least two years (a total of 730 days) during the past five year period from the date of settlement when you purchased the property. Short temporary absences, such as vacations, are counted as periods of use.

OWNERSHIP TEST

You as the taxpayer or your spouse have owned the home for two years during the past five year period. The ownership and use test can be met during different two year periods. However, both tests must be met during the five year period ending on the date of settlement for the sale of your principal residence.

> You can exclude up to $500,000 of gain if all of the following are true:
>   a) you are married and file a joint return for the year of sale.
>   b) either spouse meets the two-year ownership test
>   c) both spouses meet the two-year use test
>   d) during the past two year period, neither spouse excluded gain from the sale of another home.

A surviving spouse may exclude up to $500,000 of gain if the property is sold in the same year that the other spouse died.

It is important to recognized that the gain is excluded – not deferred – and you do not have to purchase a replacement property. You may even convert one of your rental properties into your new principal residence and start a new two year period.

Gain Not Excluded.

a) gain not excluded is any depreciation taken on the property after May 6, 1997. For instance if the house was rented, the recaptured Section 1250 depreciation will be taxed at 25%.

b) the taxpayer may not exclude the maximum amount of gain if during the previous two year period he or she sold another home and excluded all or part of that gain (See Reduced Maximum Exclusion of Gain below).

c) any portion of the gain from property (separate from the dwelling unit) not used for residential purposes may not be excluded under Section 121 (example: farm property). The portion of the property used for business or investment purposes may be exchanged and the tax deferred under Section 1031.

However, other then the recapture of depreciation taken, gain on non-residential use within a dwelling unit may be excluded. (example: a home office within the dwelling unit).

To determine the gain allocable to the residential and non-residential portions of the property, the taxpayer must allocate the basis and amount of gain realized using the same method of allocation used to determine depreciation adjustments. (See Regulation Section 1.121-1(e) for complete examples).

d) Section 1.121(d)(10) was added by Congress in October 2004 and created a five year ownership requirement if the principal residence was received in a IRC 1031 like-kind exchange. Exclusion of gain will not be allowed if the principal residence being sold was converted from a business or rental property received in a like-kind exchange and the property has not been owned for 5 years prior to the date of sale.

Additional Rules. There are some additional rules which also favor the taxpayer.

These are:

(a) If an adjoining vacant lot is sold within plus or minus two years of the settlement of the principal residence, then the total gain combined may be excluded up to the maximum allowed.

(b) In a divorce or separation, if part of the settlement, the ex-spouse owner not living in the property can claim it as his or her personal residence when the property is sold, provided the other spouse or former spouse is using the property as his or her principal residence.

(c) Residence in a licensed facility by a physical or mentally incapable person counts toward use after one year of living in the property being sold.

(d) If not remarried, a surviving spouse may use any period the deceased spouse owned and used the property as a principal residence before death.

(e) The taxpayer or spouse **does not** have to be living in the property at time of settlement to claim the exclusion. The property may be vacant or rented out.

(f) A taxpayer may exclude gain on the sale of a partial interest, if the **partial interest** sold includes an interest in the dwelling unit. Except for sales to a related party, the taxpayer may also apply the Section 121 exclusion rules when the remaining interest in the principal residence is sold.

Principal Residence Defined. Whether property is used by the taxpayer as the principal residence depends upon all the facts and circumstances. A principal residence may include a houseboat, a house trailer, or a co-op. If a taxpayer alternates between two properties, using each as a residence for successive periods of time, the property that the taxpayer uses a majority of the time during the year ordinarily will be considered the taxpayer's principal residence. In addition to the taxpayer's use of the property, relevant factors in determining a taxpayer's principal residence, include, but are not limited to—

(i) The taxpayer's place of employment; (ii) The principal place of abode of the taxpayer's family members; (iii) The address listed on the taxpayer's federal and state tax returns, driver's license, automobile registration, and voter registration card; (iv) The taxpayer's mailing address for bills and correspondence; (v) The location of the taxpayer's banks; and (vi) The location of religious organizations and recreational clubs with which the taxpayer is affiliated.

Trust and Single Member Entity Ownership. If the taxpayer is the grantor of a trust, or a single member owner of a disregarded entity for federal tax purposes (such as an LLC) and the entity owns the property, the taxpayer will be considered the owner to satisfy the two year ownership requirements.

Reduced Maximum Exclusion of Gain. If the use or ownership of the property is less than two years OR the taxpayer has excluded gain within the preceding two years, than the maximum amount of exclusion will be reduced if the primary reason for the sale is: change in place of employment, health, or unforeseen circumstances.

Place of Employment. If the primary reason for the sale is a change in **place of employment** of a **"qualified individual"** then a reduced exclusion may be claimed if employment is (1) with the same or a different employer, or (2) is new or the same self employment. The new place of employment must be 50 miles further from the residence sold than was the previous place of employment, or at least 50 miles if "qualified individual" is unemployed. See IRS Regulation Section 1.121-3(c)

Health. A reduced exclusion may be claimed if the **health** of a "qualified individual" is the primary reason for the sale. Health reasons include the need to obtain, provide for or facilitate treatment of a "qualified individual"; or if a physician recommends change of residence for health reasons. See IRS Regulation Section 1.121-3(d).

Unforeseen Circumstances. A sale is by reason of unforeseen circumstances if during the period of ownership and use as a principal residence the primary reason for the sale is the occurrence of an event that the taxpayer could not have reasonably anticipated before purchasing and occupying the residence.

Unforeseen circumstances include the involuntary conversion (condemnation), or destruction of the residence; or if involving a "Qualified Individual" — their death, loss of job if eligible for unemployment insurance, change in employment or self-employment if unable to pay housing costs, etc., divorce or legal separation, or multiple births from the same pregnancy.

Qualified Individual. The regulations significantly expand the circumstances in which the taxpayer may be able to claim an exclusion of the gain on the sale of their principal residence. A "qualified individual" is **the taxpayer, spouse, co-owner, or a person who lives with the taxpayer.** In addition, if the primary reason for the sale is health, then certain family members are also qualified individuals, including a descendant of the taxpayer's grandparent.

Computation of the Reduced Maximum Exclusion for Each Taxpayer. The amount of the exclusion that may be claimed is still very generous and for most homeowners will cover all of their capital gain.

The formula used is: divide the **lesser** of the days owned, or the days used as a primary residence, or the number of days between the date of sale (settlement or transfer) of a previous property for which the taxpayer excluded gain under Section 121 and the date of sale of the current property by 730 (the number of days in two years). This gives the percentage of days owned or used as a primary residence during the two year period. This percentage is then multiplied times $250,000 to give the maximum dollar amount of exclusion per taxpayer.

Example: The taxpayer had to move due to a job transfer after living in the house for 400 days.

Computation: 400 divided by 730 equals 55% times $250,000 equals $137,000.

Result: Up to $137,000 of capital gain may be excluded from income.

Retroactive. Most provisions of the IRS regulations are retroactive to May 7, 1997. This is the date that IRC Section 121, Exclusion of Gain from Sale of Principal Residence, was effective. Thus if you have paid capital gains tax unnecessarily on the sale of a principal residence you may file an amended income tax return and claim a refund. As always you should consult with your tax advisor.

Suspension of 5-Year Period for Military and Foreign Service Personnel. The "Military Tax Relief Act of 2003" (H.R. 3365), dated November 11, 2003, amended IRC Section 121 to suspend for a maximum of ten years the running of the five year period while the taxpayer or their spouse is "serving on qualified official extended duty as a member of the uniformed services or the Foreign Service". The term 'qualified official extended duty' means "any extended duty while serving at a duty station which is at least 50 miles from such property or while residing under Government orders in Government quarters". The term 'extended duty' means any period of active duty for a period in excess of 90 days or for an indefinite period.

Foreign Service and military personnel qualify for the exclusion of profits on their sale if they have owned and lived in the property for a period of two years over the last five years plus the period suspended while on "qualified extended official duty". The property may currently be vacant or be a rental.

To implement the law IRS Regulation Section 1.121-5 was published August 16, 2004 (T.D. 9152, 69 FR 50306). It provides the following example:

Example. B purchases a house in Virginia in 2003 that he uses as his principal residence for 3 years. For 8 years, from 2006 through 2014, B serves on qualified official extended duty as a member of the Foreign Service of the United States in Brazil. In 2015 B sells the house. B did not use the house as his principal residence for 2 of the 5 years preceding the sale. Under section 121(d)(9)and this section, however, B may elect to suspend the running of the 5-year period of ownership and use during his 8-year period of service with the Foreign Service in Brazil. If B makes the election, the 8-year period is not counted in determining whether B used the house for 2 of the 5 years preceding the sale. Therefore, B may exclude the gain from the sale of the house under section 121.

If the owner qualifies, then profit from the sale of the house up to $250,000 if single, or up to $500,000 if married and filing a joint return, will be excluded from income. The only taxable income would be the recapture of depreciation taken on the house since May 6, 1997.

The change is optional and retroactive to 1997. If a military or foreign service tax payer has paid the capital gains tax because they did not previously qualify they may file an amended return on IRS Form 1040X to obtain a refund. Even if the time period for filing an amended return for the year the tax was paid has passed, the law permitted a claim to be submitted until November 10, 2004. See IRS Regulation Section 1.121-5.

IRS Newsroom Release *IR-2003-132, Nov. 24, 2003* provides good examples and procedures for filing a refund. (See www.irs.gov/index.html)

Reference. To get all of the details and some excellent worksheets to figure the exclusion go to IRS Publication 523 "Selling Your Home". This publication is available at www.irs.gov.

For copies of the five current regulations go to the Electronic Code of Federal Regulations http://ecfr.gpoaccess.gov then select "Title 26 – Internal Revenue", then select Volume 2, Parts 1.61-1.169, then select from the Table of Contents - §1.121-1 through § 1.121-5.

Notes

Appendix

IRS Regulation for Tax Deferred Like Kind Exchanges

With revisions through February 1, 2002

SECTION 1.1031(k)-1 TREATMENT OF DEFERRED EXCHANGES.

(a) OVERVIEW. This section provides rules for the application of section 1031 and the regulations there under in the case of a "deferred exchange." For purposes of section 1031 and this section, a deferred exchange is defined as an exchange in which, pursuant to an agreement, the taxpayer transfers property held for productive use in a trade or business or for investment (the "relinquished property") and subsequently receives property to be held either for productive use in a trade or business or for investment (the "replacement property"). In the case of a deferred exchange, if the requirements set forth in paragraphs (b), (c), and (d) of this section (relating to identification and receipt of replacement property) are not satisfied, the replacement property received by the taxpayer will be treated as property which is not of a like kind to the relinquished property. In order to constitute a deferred exchange, the transaction must be an exchange (i.e., a transfer of property for property, as distinguished from a transfer of property for money). For example, a sale of property followed by a purchase of property of a like kind does not qualify for non recognition of gain or loss under section 1031 regardless of whether the identification and receipt requirements of section 1031(a)(3) and paragraphs (b), (c), and (d) of this section are satisfied. The transfer of relinquished property in a deferred exchange is not within the provisions of section 1031(a) if, as part of the consideration, the taxpayer receives money or property which does not meet the requirements of section 1031(a), but the transfer, if otherwise qualified, will be within the provisions of either section 1031(b) or (c). See section 1.1031(a)- 1(a)(2). In addition, in the case of a transfer of relinquished property in a deferred exchange, gain or loss may be recognized if the taxpayer actually or constructively receives money or property which does not meet the requirements of section 1031(a) before the taxpayer actually receives like-kind replacement property. If the taxpayer actually or constructively receives money or property which does not meet the requirements of section 1031(a) in the full amount of the consideration for the relinquished property, the transaction will constitute a sale, and not a deferred exchange, even though the taxpayer may ultimately receive like-kind replacement property. For purposes of this section, property which does not meet the requirements of section 1031(a)(whether by being described in section 1031(a)(2) or otherwise) is referred to as "other property." For rules regarding actual and constructive receipt, and safe harbors therefrom, see paragraphs (f) and (g), respectively, of this section. For rules regarding the determination of gain or loss recognized and the basis of property received in a deferred exchange, see paragraph (j) of this section.

(b) IDENTIFICATION AND RECEIPT REQUIREMENTS—

(1) IN GENERAL. In the case of a deferred exchange, any replacement property received by the taxpayer will be treated as property which is not of a like kind to the relinquished property if—

(i) The replacement property is not "identified" before the end of the "identification period," or

(ii) The identified replacement property is not received before the end of the "exchange period."

(2) IDENTIFICATION PERIOD AND EXCHANGE PERIOD.

(i) The identification period begins on the date the taxpayer transfers the relinquished property and ends at midnight on the 45th day thereafter.

(ii) The exchange period begins on the date the taxpayer transfers the relinquished property and ends at midnight on the earlier of the 180th day thereafter or the due date (including extensions) for the taxpayer's return of the tax imposed by chapter 1 of subtitle A of the Code for the taxable year in which the transfer of the relinquished property occurs.

(iii) If, as part of the same deferred exchange, the taxpayer transfers more than one relinquished property and the relinquished properties are transferred on different dates, the identification period and the exchange period are determined by reference to the earliest date on which any of the properties are transferred.

(iv) For purposes of this paragraph (b)(2), property is transferred when the property is disposed of within the meaning of section 1001(a).

(3) EXAMPLE. This paragraph (b) may be illustrated by the following example.

EXAMPLE. (i) M is a corporation that files its Federal income tax return on a calendar year basis. M and C enter into an agreement for an exchange of property that requires M to transfer property X to C. Under the agreement, M is to identify like-kind replacement property which C is required to purchase and to transfer to M. M transfers property X to C on November 16, 1992.

(ii) The identification period ends at midnight on December 31, 1992, the day which is 45 days after the date of transfer of property X. The exchange period ends at midnight on March 15, 1993, the due date for M's Federal income tax return for the taxable year in which M transferred property X. However, if M is allowed the automatic six-month extension for filing its tax return, the exchange period ends at midnight on May 15, 1993, the day which is 180 days after the date of transfer of property

(c) IDENTIFICATION OF REPLACEMENT PROPERTY BEFORE THE END OF THE IDENTIFICATION PERIOD –

(1) IN GENERAL. For purposes of paragraph (b)(1)(i) of this section (relating to the identification requirement), replacement property is identified before the end of the identification period only if the requirements of this paragraph (c) are satisfied with respect to the replacement property. However, any replacement property that is received by the taxpayer before the end of the identification period will in all events be treated as identified before the end of the identification period.

(2) MANNER OF IDENTIFYING REPLACEMENT PROPERTY. Replacement property is identified only if it is designated as replacement property in a written document signed by the taxpayer and hand delivered, mailed, telecopied, or otherwise sent before the end of the identification period to either --

(i) The person obligated to transfer the replacement property to the taxpayer (regardless of whether that person is a disqualified person as defined in paragraph (k) of this section); or

(ii) Any other person involved in the exchange other than the taxpayer or a disqualified person (as defined in paragraph (k) of this section).

Examples of persons involved in the exchange include any of the parties to the exchange, an intermediary, an escrow agent, and a title company. An identification of replacement property made in a written agreement for the exchange of properties signed by all parties thereto before the end of the identification period will be treated as satisfying the requirements of this paragraph (c)(2).

(3) DESCRIPTION OF REPLACEMENT PROPERTY. Replacement property is identified only if it is unambiguously described in the written document or agreement. Real property generally is unambiguously described if it is described by a legal description, street address, or distinguishable name (e.g., the Mayfair Apartment Building). Personal property generally is unambiguously described if it is described by a specific description of the particular type of property. For example, a truck generally is unambiguously described if it is described by a specific make, model, and year.

(4) ALTERNATIVE AND MULTIPLE PROPERTIES.

(i) The taxpayer may identify more than one replacement property. Regardless of the number of relinquished properties transferred by the taxpayer as part of the same deferred exchange, the maximum number of replacement properties that the taxpayer may identify is

(A) Three properties without regard to the fair market value of the properties (the "3-property rule"), or

(B) Any number of properties as long as their aggregate fair market value as of the end of the identification period does not exceed 200 percent of the aggregate fair market value of all the relinquished properties as of the date the relinquished properties were transferred by the taxpayer (the "200 percent rule").

(ii) If, as of the end of the identification period, the taxpayer has identified more properties as replacement properties than permitted by paragraph (c)(4)(i) of this section, the taxpayer is treated as if no replacement property had been identified. The preceding sentence will not apply, however, and an identification satisfying the requirements of paragraph (c)(4)(i) of this section will be considered made, with respect to --

(A) Any replacement property received by the taxpayer before the end of the identification period, and

(B) Any replacement property identified before the end of the identification period and received before the end of the exchange period, but only if the taxpayer receives before the end of the exchange period identified replacement property the fair market value of which is at least 95 percent of the aggregate fair market value of all identified replacement properties (the "95-percent rule").

For this purpose, the fair market value of each identified replacement property is determined as of the earlier of the date the property is received by the taxpayer or the last day of the exchange period.

(iii) For purposes of applying the 3-property rule, the 200- percent rule, and the 95-percent rule, all identifications of replacement property, other than identifications of replacement property that have been revoked in the manner provided in paragraph (c)(6) of this section, are taken into account. For example, if, in a deferred exchange, B transfers property X with a fair market value of $100,000 to C and B receives like-kind property Y with a fair market value of $50,000 before the end of the identification period, under paragraph (c)(1) of this section, property Y is treated as identified by reason of being received before the end of the identification period. Thus, under paragraph (c)(4)(i) of this section, B may identify either two additional replacement properties of any fair market value or any number of additional replacement properties as long as the aggregate fair market value of the additional replacement properties does not exceed $150,000.

(5) INCIDENTAL PROPERTY DISREGARDED.

(i) Solely for purposes of applying this paragraph (c), property that is incidental to a larger item of property is not treated as property that is separate from the larger item of property. Property is incidental to a larger item of property if --

(A) In standard commercial transactions, the property is typically transferred together with the larger item of property, and

(B) The aggregate fair market value of all of the incidental property does not exceed 15 percent of the aggregate fair market value of the larger item of property.

(ii) This paragraph (c)(5) may be illustrated by the following examples.

EXAMPLE 1. For purposes of paragraph (c) of this section, a spare tire and tool kit will not be treated as separate property from a truck with a fair market value of $10,000, if the aggregate fair market value of the spare tire and tool kit does not exceed $1,500. For purposes of the 3-property rule, the truck, spare tire, and tool kit are treated as 1 property. Moreover, for purposes of paragraph (c)(3) of this section (relating to the description of replacement property), the truck, spare tire, and tool kit are all considered to be unambiguously described if the make, model, and year of the truck are specified, even if no reference is made to the spare tire and tool kit.

EXAMPLE 2. For purposes of paragraph (c) of this section, furniture, laundry machines, and other miscellaneous items of personal property will not be treated as separate property from an apartment building with a fair-market value of $1,000,000 if the aggregate fair market value of the furniture, laundry machines, and other personal property does not exceed $150,000. For purposes of the 3-property rule, the apartment building, furniture, laundry machines, and other personal property are treated as 1 property. Moreover, for purposes of paragraph (c)(3) of this section (relating to the description of replacement property), the apartment building, furniture, laundry machines, and other personal property are all considered to be unambiguously described if the legal description, street address, or distinguishable name of the apartment building is specified, even if no reference is made to the furniture, laundry machines, and other personal property.

(6) REVOCATION OF IDENTIFICATION. An identification of replacement property may be revoked at any time before the end of the identification period. An identification of replacement property is revoked only if the revocation is made in a written document signed by the taxpayer and hand delivered, mailed, telecopied, or otherwise sent before the end of the identification period to the person to whom the identification of the replacement property was sent. An identification of replacement property that is made in a written agreement for the exchange of properties is treated as revoked only if the revocation is made in a written amendment to the agreement or in a written document signed by the taxpayer and hand delivered, mailed, telecopied, or otherwise sent before the end of the identification period to all of the parties to the agreement.

(7) EXAMPLES. This paragraph (c) may be illustrated by the following examples. Unless otherwise provided in an example, the following facts are assumed: B, a calendar year taxpayer, and C agree to enter into a deferred exchange. Pursuant to their agreement, B transfers real property X to C on May 17, 1991. Real property X, which has been held by B for investment, is unencumbered and has a fair market value

on May 17, 1991, of $100,000. On or before July 1, 1991 (the end of the identification period), B is to identify replacement property that is of a like kind to real property X. On or before November 13, 1991 (the end of the exchange period), C is required to purchase the property identified by B and to transfer that property to B. To the extent the fair market value of the replacement property transferred to B is greater or less than the fair market value of real property X, either B or C, as applicable, will make up the difference by paying cash to the other party after the date the replacement property is received by B. No replacement property is identified in the agreement. When subsequently identified, the replacement property is described by legal description and is of a like kind to real property X (determined without regard to section 1031(a)(3) and this section). B intends to hold the replacement property received for investment.

EXAMPLE 1. (i) On July 2, 1991, B identifies real property E as replacement property by designating real property E as replacement property in a written document signed by B and personally delivered to C.

(ii) Because the identification was made after the end of the identification period, pursuant to paragraph (b)(1)(i) of this section (relating to the identification requirement), real property E is treated as property which is not of a like kind to real property X.

EXAMPLE 2. (i) C is a corporation of which 20 percent of the outstanding stock is owned by B. On July 1, 1991, B identifies real property F as replacement property by designating real property F as replacement property in a written document signed by B and mailed to C.

(ii) Because C is the person obligated to transfer the replacement property to B, real property F is identified before the end of the identification period. The fact that C is a "disqualified person" as defined in paragraph (k) of this section does not change this result.

(iii) Real property F would also have been treated as identified before the end of the identification period if, instead of sending the identification to C, B had designated real property F as replacement property in a written agreement for the exchange of properties signed by all parties thereto on or before July 1, 1991.

EXAMPLE 3. (i) On June 3, 1991, B identifies the replacement property as "unimproved land located in Hood County with a fair market value not to exceed $100,000." The designation is made in a written document signed by B and personally delivered to C. On July 8, 1991, B and C agree that real property G is the property described in the June 3, 1991 document.

(ii) Because real property G was not unambiguously described before the end of the identification period, no replacement property is identified before the end of the identification period.

EXAMPLE 4. (i) On June 28, 1991, B identifies real properties H, J, and K as replacement properties by designating these properties as replacement properties in a written document signed by B and personally delivered to C. The written document provides that by August 1, 1991, B will orally inform C which of the identified properties C is to transfer to B. As of July 1, 1991, the fair market values of real properties H, J, and K are $75,000, $100,000, and $125,000, respectively.

(ii) Because B did not identify more than three properties as replacement properties, the requirements of the 3-property rule are satisfied, and real properties H, J, and K are all identified before the end of the identification period.

EXAMPLE 5. (i) On May 17, 1991, B identifies real properties L, M, N, and P as replacement properties by designating these properties as replacement properties in a written document signed by B and personally delivered to C. The written document provides that by July 2, 1991, B will orally inform C which of the identified properties C is to transfer to B. As of July 1, 1991, the fair market values of real properties L, M, N, and P are $30,000, $40,000, $50,000, and $60,000, respectively.

(ii) Although B identified more than three properties as replacement properties, the aggregate fair market value of the identified properties as of the end of the identification period ($180,000) did not exceed 200 percent of the aggregate fair market value of real property X (200% x $100,000 = $200,000). Therefore, the requirements of the 200-percent rule are satisfied, and real properties L, M, N, and P are all identified before the end of the identification period.

EXAMPLE 6. (i) On June 21, 1991, B identifies real properties Q, R, and S as replacement properties by designating these properties as replacement properties in a written document signed by B and mailed to C. On June 24, 1991, B identifies real properties T and U as replacement properties in a written document signed by B and mailed to C. On June 28, 1991, B revokes the identification of real properties Q and R in a written document signed by B and personally delivered to C.

(ii) B has revoked the identification of real properties Q and R in the manner provided by paragraph (c)(6) of this section. Identifications of replacement property that have been revoked in the manner provided by paragraph (c)(6) of this section are not taken into account for purposes of applying the 3-property rule. Thus, as of June 28, 1991, B has identified only replacement properties S, T, and U for purposes of the 3 property rule. Because B did not identify more than three properties as replacement properties for purposes of the 3 property rule, the requirements of that rule are satisfied, and real properties S, T, and U are all identified before the end of the identification period.

EXAMPLE 7. (i) On May 20, 1991, B identifies real properties V and W as replacement properties by designating these properties as replacement properties in a written document signed by B and personally delivered to C. On June 4, 1991, B identifies real properties Y and Z as replacement properties in the same manner. On June 5, 1991, B telephones C and orally revokes the identification of real properties V and W. As of July 1, 1991, the fair market values of real properties V, W, Y, and Z are $50,000, $70,000, $90,000, and $100,000, respectively. On July 31, 1991, C purchases real property Y and Z and transfers them to B.

(ii) Pursuant to paragraph (c)(6) of this section (relating to revocation of identification), the oral revocation of the identification of real properties V and W is invalid. Thus, the identification of real properties V and W is taken into account for purposes of determining whether the requirements of paragraph (c)(4) of this section (relating to the identification of alternative and multiple properties) are satisfied. Because B identified more than three properties and the aggregate fair market value of the identified properties as of the end of the identification period ($310,000) exceeds 200 percent of the fair market value of real property X (200% x $100,000 = $200,000), the requirements of paragraph (c)(4) of this section are not satisfied, and B is treated as if B did not identify any replacement property.

(d) RECEIPT OF IDENTIFIED REPLACEMENT PROPERTY –

(1) IN GENERAL. For purposes of paragraph (b)(1)(ii) of this section (relating to the receipt requirement), the identified replacement property is received before the end of the exchange period

only if the requirements of this paragraph (d) are satisfied with respect to the replacement property. In the case of a deferred exchange, the identified replacement property is received before the end of the exchange period if --

(i) The taxpayer receives the replacement property before the end of the exchange period, and

(ii) The replacement property received is substantially the same property as identified.

If the taxpayer has identified more than one replacement property, section 1031(a)(3)(B) and this paragraph (d) are applied separately to each replacement property.

(2) EXAMPLES. This paragraph (d) may be illustrated by the following examples. The following facts are assumed: B, a calendar year taxpayer, and C agree to enter into a deferred exchange. Pursuant to their agreement, B transfers real property X to C on May 17, 1991. Real property X, which has been held by B for investment, is unencumbered and has a fair market value on May 17, 1991, of $100,000. On or before July 1, 1991 (the end of the identification period), B is to identify replacement property that is of a like kind to real property X. On or before November 13, 1991 (the end of the exchange period), C is required to purchase the property identified by B and to transfer that property to B. To the extent the fair market value of the replacement property transferred to B is greater or less than the fair market value of real property X, either B or C, as applicable, will make up the difference by paying cash to the other party after the date the replacement property is received by B. The replacement property is identified in a manner that satisfies paragraph (c) of this section (relating to identification of replacement property) and is of a like kind to real property X (determined without regard to section 1031(a)(3) and this section). B intends to hold any replacement property received for investment.

EXAMPLE 1. (i) In the agreement, B identifies real properties J, K, and L as replacement properties. The agreement provides that by July 26, 1991, B will orally inform C which of the properties C is to transfer to B.

(ii) As of July 1, 1991, the fair market values of real properties J, K, and L are $75,000, $100,000, and $125,000, respectively. On July 26, 1991, B instructs C to acquire real property X. On October 31, 1991, C purchases real property K for $100,000 and transfers the property to B.

(iii) Because real property K was identified before the end of the identification period and was received before the end of the exchange period, the identification and receipt requirements of section 1031(a)(3) and this section are satisfied with respect to real property K.

EXAMPLE 2. (i) In the agreement, B identifies real property P as replacement property. Real property P consists of two acres of unimproved land. On October 15, 1991, the owner of real property P erects a fence on the property. On November 1, 1991, C purchases real property P and transfers it to B.

(ii) The erection of the fence on real property P subsequent to its identification did not alter the basic nature or character of real property P as unimproved land. B is considered to have received substantially the same property as identified.

EXAMPLE 3. (i) In the agreement, B identifies real property Q as replacement property. Real property Q consists of a barn on two acres of land and has a fair market value of $250,000 ($187,500 for the barn and underlying land and $87,500 for the remaining land). As of July 26, 1991, real property Q remains unchanged and has a fair market value of $250,000. On that date, at B's direction, C purchases the barn and underlying land for $187,500 and transfers it to B, and B pays $87,500 to C.

(ii) The barn and underlying land differ in basic nature or character from real property Q as a whole. B is not considered to have received substantially the same property as identified.

EXAMPLE 4. (i) In the agreement, B identifies real property R as replacement property. Real property R consists of two acres of unimproved land and has a fair market value of $250,000. As of October 3, 1991, real property R remains unimproved and has a fair market value of $250,000. On that date, at B's direction, C purchases 1 ½ acres of real property R for $187,500 and transfers it to B, and B pays $87,500 to C.

(ii) The portion of real property R that B received does not differ from the basic nature or character of real property R as a whole. Moreover, the fair market value of the portion of real property R that B received ($187,500) is 75 percent of the fair market value of real property R as of the date of receipt. Accordingly, B is considered to have received substantially the same property as identified.

(e) SPECIAL RULES FOR IDENTIFICATION AND RECEIPT OF REPLACEMENT PROPERTY TO BE PRODUCED—

(1) IN GENERAL. A transfer of relinquished property in a deferred exchange will not fail to qualify for non recognition of gain or loss under section 1031 merely because the replacement property is not in existence or is being produced at the time the property is identified as replacement property. For purposes of this paragraph (e), the terms "produced" and "production" have the same meanings as provided in section 263A(g)(1) and the regulations there under.

(2) IDENTIFICATION OF REPLACEMENT PROPERTY TO BE PRODUCED.

(i) In the case of replacement property that is to be produced, the replacement property must be identified as provided in paragraph (c) of this section (relating to identification of replacement property). For example, if the identified replacement property consists of improved real property where the improvements are to be constructed, the description of the replacement property satisfies the requirements of paragraph (c)(3) of this section (relating to description of replacement property) if a legal description is provided for the underlying land and as much detail is provided regarding construction of the improvements as is practicable at the time the identification is made.

(ii) For purposes of paragraphs (c)(4)(i)(B) and (c)(5) of this section (relating to the 200-percent rule and incidental property), the fair market value of replacement property that is to be produced is its estimated fair market value as of the date it is expected to be received by the taxpayer.

(3) RECEIPT OF REPLACEMENT PROPERTY TO BE PRODUCED.

(i) For purposes of paragraph (d)(1)(ii) of this section (relating to receipt of the identified replacement property), in determining whether the replacement property received by the taxpayer is substantially the same property as identified where the identified replacement property is property to be produced, variations due to usual or typical production changes are not taken into account. However, if substantial changes are made in the property to be produced, the replacement property received will not be considered to be substantially the same property as identified.

(ii) If the identified replacement property is personal property to be produced, the replacement property received will not be considered to be substantially the same property as identified unless production of the replacement property received is completed on or before the date the property is received by the taxpayer.

(iii) If the identified replacement property is real property to be produced and the production of the property is not completed on or before the date the taxpayer receives the property, the property received will be considered to be substantially the same property as identified only if, had production been completed on or before the date the taxpayer receives the replacement property, the property received would have been considered to be substantially the same property as identified. Even so, the property received is considered to be substantially the same property as identified only to the extent the property received constitutes real property under local law.

(4) ADDITIONAL RULES. The transfer of relinquished property is not within the provisions of section 1031 (a) if the relinquished property is transferred in exchange for services (including production services). Thus, any additional production occurring with respect to the replacement property after the property is received by the taxpayer will not be treated as the receipt of property of a like kind.

(5) EXAMPLE. This paragraph (e) may be illustrated by the following example.

EXAMPLE. (i) B, a calendar year taxpayer, and C agree to enter into a deferred exchange. Pursuant to their agreement, B transfers improved real property X and personal property Y to C on May 17, 1991. On or before November 13, 1991 (the end of the exchange period), C is required to transfer to B real property M, on which C is constructing improvements, and personal property N, which C is producing. C is obligated to complete the improvements and production regardless of when properties M and N are transferred to B. Properties M and N are identified in a manner that satisfies paragraphs (c) (relating to identification of replacement property) and (e)(2) of this section. In addition, properties M and N are of a like kind, respectively, to real property X and personal property Y (determined without regard to section 1031(a)(3) and this section). On November 13, 1991, when construction of the improvements to property M is 20 percent completed and the production of property N is 90 percent completed, C transfers to B property M and property N. If construction of the improvements had been completed, property M would have been considered to be substantially the same property as identified. Under local law, property M constitutes real property to the extent of the underlying land and the 20 percent of the construction that is completed.

(ii) Because property N is personal property to be produced and production of property N is not completed before the date the property is received by B, property N is not considered to be substantially the same property as identified and is treated as property which is not of a like kind to property Y.

(iii) Property M is considered to be substantially the same property as identified to the extent of the underlying land and the 20 percent of the construction that is completed when property M is received by B. However, any additional construction performed by C with respect to property M after November 13, 1991, is not treated as the receipt of property of a like kind.

(f) RECEIPT OF MONEY OR OTHER PROPERTY –

(1) IN GENERAL. A transfer of relinquished property in a deferred exchange is not within the provisions of section 1031(a) if, as part of the consideration, the taxpayer receives money or other property. However, such a transfer, if otherwise qualified, will be within the provisions of either section 1031(b) or (c). See section 1.1031(a)- 1(a)(2). In addition, in the case of a transfer of relinquished property in a deferred exchange, gain or loss may be recognized if the taxpayer actually or constructively receives money or other property before the taxpayer actually receives like-kind replacement property. If the taxpayer actually or constructively receives money or other property in the full amount of the consideration for the relinquished property before the taxpayer actually receives like-kind replacement property, the transaction will constitute a sale and not a deferred exchange, even though the taxpayer may ultimately receive like-kind replacement property.

(2) ACTUAL AND CONSTRUCTIVE RECEIPT. Except as provided in paragraph (g) of this section (relating to safe harbors), for purposes of section 1031 and this section, the determination of whether (or the extent to which) the taxpayer is in actual or constructive receipt of money or other property before the taxpayer actually receives like-kind replacement property is made under the general rules concerning actual and constructive receipt and without regard to the taxpayer's method of accounting. The taxpayer is in actual receipt of money or property at the time the taxpayer actually receives the money or property or receives the economic benefit of the money or property. The taxpayer is in constructive receipt of money or property at the time the money or property is credited to the taxpayer's account, set apart for the taxpayer, or otherwise made available so that the taxpayer may draw upon it at any time or so that the taxpayer can draw upon it if notice of intention to draw is given. Although the taxpayer is not in constructive receipt of money or property if the taxpayer's control of its receipt is subject to substantial limitations or restrictions, the taxpayer is in constructive receipt of the money or property at the time the limitations or restrictions lapse, expire, or are waived. In addition, actual or constructive receipt of money or property by an agent of the taxpayer (determined without regard to paragraph (k) of this section) is actual or constructive receipt by the taxpayer.

(3) EXAMPLE. This paragraph (f) may be illustrated by the following example.

EXAMPLE. (i) B, a calendar year taxpayer, and C agree to enter into a deferred exchange. Pursuant to the agreement, on May 17, 1991, B transfers real property X to C. Real property X, which has been held by B for investment, is unencumbered and has a fair market value on May 17, 1991, of $100,000. On or before July 1, 1991 (the end of the identification period), B is to identify replacement property that is of a like kind to real property X. On or before November 13, 1991 (the end of the exchange period), C is required to purchase the property identified by B and to transfer that property to B. At any time after May 17, 1991, and before C has purchased the replacement property, B has the right, upon notice, to demand that C pay $100,000 in lieu of acquiring and transferring the replacement property. Pursuant to the agreement, B identifies replacement property, and C purchases the replacement property and transfers it to B.

(ii) Under the agreement, B has the unrestricted right to demand the payment of $100,000 as of May 17, 1991. B is therefore in constructive receipt of $100,000 on that date. Because B is in constructive receipt of money in the full amount of the consideration for the relinquished property before B actually receives the like-kind replacement property, the transaction constitutes a sale, and the transfer of real property X does not qualify for nonrecognition of gain or loss under section 1031. B is treated as if B received the $100,000 in consideration for the sale of real property X and then purchased the like-kind replacement property.

(iii) If B's right to demand payment of the $100,000 were subject to a substantial limitation or restriction (e.g., the agreement provided that B had no right to demand payment before November 14, 1991 (the end of the exchange period)), then, for purposes of this section, B would not be in actual or constructive receipt of the money unless (or until) the limitation or restriction lapsed, expired, or was waived.

(g) SAFE HARBORS –

(1) IN GENERAL. Paragraphs (g)(2) through (g)(5) of this section set forth four safe harbors the use of which will result in a determination that the taxpayer is not in actual or constructive receipt of money or other property for purposes of section 1031 and this section. More than one safe harbor can be used in the same deferred exchange, but the terms and conditions of each must be separately satisfied. For purposes of the safe harbor rules, the term "taxpayer" does not include a person or entity utilized in a safe harbor (e.g., a qualified intermediary). See paragraph (g)(8), Example 3 (v), of this section.

(2) SECURITY OR GUARANTEE ARRANGEMENTS.

(i) In the case of a deferred exchange, the determination of whether the taxpayer is in actual or constructive receipt of money or other property before the taxpayer actually receives like-kind replacement property will be made without regard to the fact that the obligation of the taxpayer's transferee to transfer the replacement property to the taxpayer is or may be secured or guaranteed by one or more of the following:

(A) A mortgage, deed of trust, or other security interest in property (other than cash or a cash equivalent),

(B) A standby letter of credit which satisfies all of the requirements of section 15A.453-1(b)(3)(iii) and which may not be drawn upon in the absence of a default of the transferee's obligation to transfer like-kind replacement property to the taxpayer, or

(C) A guarantee of a third party.

(ii) Paragraph (g)(2)(i) of this section ceases to apply at the time the taxpayer has an immediate ability or unrestricted right to receive money or other property pursuant to the security or guarantee arrangement.

(3) QUALIFIED ESCROW ACCOUNTS AND QUALIFIED TRUSTS.

(i) In the case of a deferred exchange, the determination of whether the taxpayer is in actual or constructive receipt of money or other property before the taxpayer actually receives like-kind replacement property will be made without regard to the fact that the obligation of the taxpayer's transferee to transfer the replacement property to the taxpayer is or may be secured by cash or a cash equivalent if the cash or cash equivalent is held in a qualified escrow account or in a qualified trust.

(ii) A qualified escrow account is an escrow account wherein --

(A) The escrow holder is not the taxpayer or a disqualified person (as defined in paragraph (k) of this section), and

(B) The escrow agreement expressly limits the taxpayer's rights to receive, pledge, borrow, or otherwise obtain the benefits of the cash or cash equivalent held in the escrow account as provided in paragraph (g)(6) of this section.

(iii) A qualified trust is a trust wherein --

(A) The trustee is not the taxpayer or a disqualified person (as defined in paragraph (k) of this section, except that for this purpose the relationship between the taxpayer and the trustee created by the qualified trust will not be considered a relationship under section 267(b)), and

(B) The trust agreement expressly limits the taxpayer's rights to receive, pledge, borrow, or otherwise obtain the benefits of the cash or cash equivalent held by the trustee as provided in paragraph (g)(6) of this section.

(iv) Paragraph (g)(3)(i) of this section ceases to apply at the time the taxpayer has an immediate ability or unrestricted right to receive, pledge, borrow, or otherwise obtain the benefits of the cash or cash equivalent held in the qualified escrow account or qualified trust. Rights conferred upon the taxpayer under state law to terminate or dismiss the escrow holder of a qualified escrow account or the trustee of a qualified trust are disregarded for this purpose.

(v) A taxpayer may receive money or other property directly from a party to the exchange, but not from a qualified escrow account or a qualified trust, without affecting the application of paragraph (g)(3)(i) of this section.

(4) QUALIFIED INTERMEDIARIES.

(i) In the case of a taxpayer's transfer of relinquished property involving a qualified intermediary, the qualified intermediary is not considered the agent of the taxpayer for purposes of section 1031(a). In such a case, the taxpayer's transfer of relinquished property and subsequent receipt of like-kind replacement property is treated as an exchange, and the determination of whether the taxpayer is in actual or constructive receipt of money or other property before the taxpayer actually receives like-kind replacement property is made as if the qualified intermediary is not the agent of the taxpayer.

(ii) Paragraph (g)(4)(i) of this section applies only if the agreement between the taxpayer and the qualified intermediary expressly limits the taxpayer's rights to receive, pledge, borrow, or otherwise obtain the benefits of money or other property held by the qualified intermediary as provided in paragraph (g)(6) of this section.

(iii) A qualified intermediary is a person who

(A) Is not the taxpayer or a disqualified person (as defined in paragraph (k) of this section), and

(B) Enters into a written agreement with the taxpayer (the "exchange agreement") and, as required by the exchange agreement, acquires the relinquished property from the taxpayer, transfers the relinquished property, acquires the replacement property, and transfers the replacement property to the taxpayer.

(iv) Regardless of whether an intermediary acquires and transfers property under general tax principals, solely for purposes of paragraph (g)(4)(iii)(B) of this section --

(A) An intermediary is treated as acquiring and transferring property if the intermediary acquires and transfers legal title to that property,

(B) An intermediary is treated as acquiring and transferring the relinquished property if the intermediary (either on its own behalf or as the agent of any party to the transaction) enters into an agreement with a person other than the taxpayer for the transfer of the relinquished property to that person and, pursuant to that agreement, the relinquished property is transferred to that person, and

(C) An intermediary is treated as acquiring and transferring replacement property if the intermediary (either on its own behalf or as the agent of any party to the transaction) enters into an agreement with the owner of the replacement property for the transfer of that property and, pursuant to that agreement, the replacement property is transferred to the taxpayer.

(v) Solely for purposes of paragraphs (g)(4)(iii) and (g)(4)(iv) of this section, an intermediary is treated as entering into an agreement if the rights of a party to the agreement are assigned to the intermediary and all parties to that agreement are notified in writing of the assignment on or before the date of the relevant transfer of property. For example, if a taxpayer enters into an agreement for the transfer of relinquished property and thereafter assigns its rights in that agreement to an intermediary and all parties to that agreement are notified in writing of the assignment on or before the date of the transfer of the relinquished property, the intermediary is treated as entering into that agreement. If the relinquished property is transferred pursuant to that agreement, the intermediary is treated as having acquired and transferred the relinquished property.

(vi) Paragraph (g)(4)(i) of this section ceases to apply at the time the taxpayer has an immediate ability or unrestricted right to receive, pledge, borrow, or otherwise obtain the benefits of money or other property held by the qualified intermediary. Rights conferred upon the taxpayer under state law to terminate or dismiss the qualified intermediary are disregarded for this purpose.

(vii) A taxpayer may receive money or other property directly from a party to the transaction other than the qualified intermediary without affecting the application of paragraph (g)(4)(i) of this section.

(5) INTEREST AND GROWTH FACTORS. In the case of a deferred exchange, the determination of whether the taxpayer is in actual or constructive receipt of money or other property before the taxpayer actually receives the like-kind replacement property will be made without regard to the fact that the taxpayer is or may be entitled to receive any interest or growth factor with respect to the deferred exchange. The preceding sentence applies only if the agreement pursuant to which the taxpayer is or may be entitled to the interest growth factor expressly limits the taxpayer's rights to receive the interest or growth factor as provided in paragraph (g)(6) of this section. For additional rules concerning interest or growth factors, see paragraph (h) of this section.

(6) ADDITIONAL RESTRICTIONS ON SAFE HARBORS UNDER PARAGRAPHS (g)(3) THROUGH (g)(5).

(i) An agreement limits a taxpayer's rights as provided in this paragraph (g)(6) only if the agreement provides that the taxpayer has no rights, except as provided in paragraphs (g)(6)(ii) and (g)(6)(iii) of this section, to receive, pledge, borrow, or otherwise obtain the benefits of money or other property before the end of the exchange period.

(ii) The agreement may provide that if the taxpayer has not identified replacement property by the end of the identification period, the taxpayer may have rights to receive, pledge, borrow, or otherwise obtain the benefits of money or other property at any time after the end of the identification period.

(iii) The agreement may provide that if the taxpayer has identified replacement property, the taxpayer may have rights to receive, pledge, borrow, or otherwise obtain the benefits of money or other property upon or after—-

(A) The receipt by the taxpayer of all of the replacement property to which the taxpayer is entitled under the exchange agreement, or

(B) The occurrence after the end of the identification period of a material and substantial contingency that—

(1) Relates to the deferred exchange,

(2) Is provided for in writing, and

(3) Is beyond the control of the taxpayer and of any disqualified person (as defined in paragraph (k) of this section), other than the person obligated to transfer the replacement property to the taxpayer.

(7) ITEMS DISREGARDED IN APPLYING SAFE HARBORS UNDER PARAGRAPHS (g)(3) THROUGH (g)(5). In determining whether a safe harbor under paragraphs (g)(3) through (g)(5) of this section ceases to apply and whether the taxpayer's rights to receive, pledge, borrow, or otherwise obtain the benefits of money or other property are expressly limited as provided in paragraph (g)(6) of this section, the taxpayer's receipt of or right to receive any of the following items will be disregarded --

(i) Items that a seller may receive as a consequence of the disposition of property and that are not included in the amount realized from the disposition of property (e.g., prorated rents), and

(ii) Transactional items that relate to the disposition of the relinquished property or to the acquisition of the replacement property and appear under local standards in the typical closing statement as the responsibility of a buyer or seller (e.g., commissions, prorated taxes, recording or transfer taxes, and title company fees).

(8) EXAMPLES. This paragraph (g) may be illustrated by the following examples. Unless otherwise provided in an example, the following facts are assumed: B, a calendar year taxpayer, and C agree to enter into a deferred exchange. Pursuant to their agreement, B is to transfer real property X to C on May 17, 1991. Real property X, which has been held by B for investment, is unencumbered and has a fair market value on May 17, 1991, of $100,000. On or before July 1, 1991 (the end of the identification period), B is to identify replacement property that is of a like kind to real property X. On or before November 13, 1991 (the end of the exchange period), C is required to purchase the property identified by B and to transfer that property to B. To the extent the fair market value of the replacement property transferred to B is greater or less than the fair market value of real property X, either B or C, as applicable, will make up the difference by paying cash to the other party after the date the replacement property is received by B. The replacement property is identified as provided in paragraph (c) of this section (relating to identification of replacement property) and is of a like kind to real property X (determined without regard to section 1031(a)(3) and this section). B intends to hold any replacement property received for investment.

EXAMPLE 1. (i) On May 17, 1991, B transfers real property X to C. On the same day, C pays $10,000 to B and deposits $90,000 in escrow as security for C's obligation to perform under the agreement. The escrow agreement provides that B has no rights to receive, pledge, borrow, or otherwise obtain the benefits of the money in escrow before November 14, 1991, except that:

(A) If B fails to identify replacement property on or before July 1, 1991, B may demand the funds in escrow at any time after July 1, 1991; and

(B) If B identifies and receives replacement property, then B may demand the balance of the remaining funds in escrow at any time after B has received the replacement property.

The funds in escrow may be used to purchase the replacement property. The escrow holder is not a disqualified person as defined in paragraph (k) of this section. Pursuant to the terms of the agreement, B identifies replacement property, and C purchases the replacement property using the funds in escrow and transfers the replacement property to B.

(ii) C's obligation to transfer the replacement property to B was secured by cash held in a qualified escrow account because the escrow holder was not a disqualified person and the escrow agreement expressly limited B's rights to receive, pledge, borrow, or otherwise obtain the benefits of the money in escrow as provided in paragraph (g)(6) of this section. In addition, B did not have the immediate ability or unrestricted right to receive money or other property in escrow before B actually received the like-kind replacement property. Therefore, for purposes of section 1031 and this section, B is determined not to be in actual or constructive receipt of the $90,000 held in escrow before B received the like-kind replacement property. The transfer of real property X by B and B's acquisition of the replacement property qualify as an exchange under section 1031. See paragraph (j) of this section for determining the amount of gain or loss recognized.

EXAMPLE 2. (i) On May 17, 1991, B transfers real property X to C, and C deposits $100,000 in escrow as security for C's obligation to perform under the agreement. Also on May 17, B identifies real property J as replacement property. The escrow agreement provides that no funds may be paid out without prior written approval of both B and C. The escrow agreement also provides that B has no rights to receive, pledge, borrow, or otherwise obtain the benefits of the money in escrow before November 14, 1991, except that:

(A) B may demand the funds in escrow at any time after the later of July 1, 1991, and the occurrence of any of the following events --

(1) real property J is destroyed, seized, requisitioned, or condemned, or

(2) a determination is made that the regulatory approval necessary for the transfer of real property J cannot be obtained in time for real property J to be transferred to B before the end of the exchange period;

(B) B may demand the funds in escrow at any time after August 14, 1991, if real property J has not been rezoned from residential to commercial use by that date; and

(C) B may demand the funds in escrow at the time B receives real property J or any time thereafter.

Otherwise, B is entitled to all funds in escrow after November 13, 1991. The funds in escrow may be used to purchase the replacement property. The escrow holder is not a disqualified person as described in paragraph (k) of this section. Real property J is not rezoned from residential to commercial use on or before August 14, 1991.

(ii) C's obligation to transfer the replacement property to B was secured by cash held in a qualified escrow account because the escrow holder was not a disqualified person and the escrow agreement expressly limited B's rights to receive, pledge, borrow, or otherwise obtain the benefits of the money in escrow as provided in paragraph (g)(6) of this section. From May 17, 1991, until August 15, 1991, B did not have the immediate ability or unrestricted right to-receive money or other property before B actually received the like-kind replacement property. Therefore, for purposes of section 1031 and this section, B is determined not to be in actual or constructive receipt of the $100,000 in escrow from May 17, 1991, until August 15, 1991. However, on August 15, 1991, B had the unrestricted right, upon notice, to draw upon the $100,000 held in escrow. Thus, the safe harbor ceased to apply and B was in constructive receipt of the funds held in escrow. Because B constructively received the full amount of the consideration ($100,000) before B actually received the like-kind replacement property, the transaction is treated as a sale and not as a deferred exchange. The result does not change even if B chose not to demand the funds in escrow and continued to attempt to have real property J rezoned and to receive the property on or before November 13, 1991.

(iii) If real property J had been rezoned on or before August 14, 1991, and C had purchased real property J and transferred it to B on or before November 13, 1991, the transaction would have qualified for non recognition of gain or loss under section 1031 (a).

EXAMPLE 3. (i) On May 1, 1991, D offers to purchase real property X for $100,000. However, D is unwilling to participate in a like-kind exchange. B thus enters into an exchange agreement with C whereby B retains C to facilitate an exchange with respect to real property X. C is not a disqualified person as described in paragraph (k) of this section. The exchange agreement between B and C provides that B is to execute and deliver a deed conveying real property X to C who, in turn, is to execute and deliver a deed conveying real property X to D. The exchange agreement expressly limits B's rights to receive, pledge, borrow, or otherwise obtain the benefits of money or other property held by C as provided in paragraph (g)(6) of this section. On May 3, 1991, C enters into an agreement with B to transfer real property X to D for $100,000. On May 17, 1991, B executes and delivers to C a deed conveying real property X to C. On the same date, C executes and delivers to D a deed conveying real property X to D, and D deposits $100,000 in escrow. The escrow holder is not a disqualified person as defined in paragraph (k) of this section and the escrow agreement expressly limits B's rights to receive, pledge, borrow, or otherwise obtain the benefits of money or other property in escrow as provided in paragraph (g)(6) of this section. However, the escrow agreement provides that the money in escrow may be used to purchase replacement property. On June 3, 1991, B identifies real property K as replacement property. On August 9, 1991, E executes and delivers to C a deed conveying real property K to C and $80,000 is released from the escrow and paid to E. On the same date, C executes and delivers to B a deed conveying real property K to B, and the escrow holder pays B $20,000, the balance of the $100,000 sale price of real property X remaining after the purchase of real property K for $80,000.

(ii) B and C entered into an exchange agreement that satisfied the requirements of paragraph (g)(4)(iii)(B) of this section. Regardless of whether C may have acquired and transferred real property X under general tax principles, C is treated as having acquired and transferred real property X because C acquired and transferred legal title to real property X. Similarly, C is treated as having acquired and transferred real property X because C acquired and transferred legal title to real property K. Thus, C was a qualified intermediary. This result is reached for purposes of this section regardless of whether C was B's agent under state law.

(iii) Because the escrow holder was not a disqualified person and the escrow agreement expressly limited B's rights to receive, pledge, borrow, or otherwise obtain the benefits of money or other property in escrow as provided in paragraph (g)(6) of this section, the escrow account was a qualified escrow account. For purposes of section 1031 and this section, therefore, B is determined not to be in actual or constructive receipt of the funds in escrow before B received real property K.

(iv) The exchange agreement between B and C expressly limited B's rights to receive, pledge, borrow, or otherwise obtain the benefits of any money held by C as provided in paragraph (g)(6) of this section. Because C was a qualified intermediary, for purposes of section 1031 and this section B is determined not to be in actual or constructive receipt of any funds held by C before B received real property K. In addition, B's transfer of real property X and acquisition of real property K qualify as an exchange under section 1031. See paragraph (j) of this section for determining the amount of gain or loss recognized.

(v) If the escrow agreement had expressly limited C's rights to receive, pledge, borrow, or otherwise obtain the benefits of money or other property in escrow as provided in paragraph (g)(6) of this section, but had not expressly limited B's rights to receive, pledge, borrow, or otherwise obtain the benefits of that money or other property, the escrow account would not have been a qualified escrow account. Consequently, paragraph (g)(3)(i) of this section would not have been applicable in determining whether B was in actual or constructive receipt of that money or other property before B received real property K.

> EXAMPLE 4. (i) On May 1, 1991, B enters into an agreement to sell real property X to D for $100,000 on May 17, 1991. However, D is unwilling to participate in a like-kind exchange. B thus enters into an exchange agreement with C whereby B retains C to facilitate an exchange with respect to real property X. C is not a disqualified person as described in paragraph (k) of this section. In the exchange agreement between B and C, B assigns to C all of B's rights in the agreement with D. The exchange agreement expressly limits B' s rights to receive, pledge, borrow, or otherwise obtain the benefits of money or other property held by C as provided in paragraph (g) (6) of this section. On May 17, 1991, B notifies D in writing of the assignment. On the same date, B executes and delivers to B a deed conveying real property X to D. D pays $10,000 to B and $90,000 to C. On June 1, 1991, B identifies real property L as replacement property . On July 5, 1991, B enters into an agreement to purchase real property L from E for $90,000, assigns its rights in that agreement to C, and notifies E in writing of the assignment. On August 9, 1991, C pays $90,000 to E, and E executes and delivers to B a deed conveying real property L to B.

(ii) The exchange agreement entered into by B and C satisfied the requirements of paragraph (g)(4)(iii)(B) of this section. Because B's rights in its agreements with D and E were assigned to C, and D and E were notified in writing of the assignment on or before the transfer of real properties X and L, respectively, C is treated as entering into those agreements. Because C is treated as entering into an agreement with D for the transfer of real property X and, pursuant to that agreement, real property X was transferred to B, C is treated as acquiring and transferring real property X. Similarly, because C is treated as entering into an agreement with E for the transfer of real property K and, pursuant to that agreement, real property K was transferred to B, C is treated as acquiring and transferring real property K. This result is reached for purposes of this section regardless of whether C was B's agent under state law and regardless of whether C is considered, under general tax principles, to have acquired title or beneficial ownership of the properties. Thus, C was a qualified intermediary.

(iii) The exchange agreement between B and C expressly limited B's rights to receive, pledge, borrow, or otherwise obtain the benefits of the money held by C as provided in paragraph (g)(6) of this section. Thus, B did not have the immediate ability or unrestricted right to receive money or other property held by C before B received real property L. For purposes of section 1031 and this section, therefore, B is determined not to be in actual or constructive receipt of the $90,000 held by C before B received real property L. In addition, the transfer of real property X by B and B's acquisition of real property L qualify as an exchange under section 1031. See paragraph (j) of this section for determining the amount of gain or loss recognized.

EXAMPLE 5. (i) On May 1, 1991, B enters into an agreement to sell real property X to B for $100,000 . However, D is unwilling to participate in a like-kind exchange. B thus enters into an agreement with C whereby B retains C to facilitate an exchange with respect to real property X. C is not a disqualified person as described in paragraph (k) of this section. The agreement between B and C expressly limits B's rights to receive, pledge, borrow, or otherwise obtain the benefits of money or other property held by C as provided in paragraph (g)(6) of this section. C neither enters into an agreement with D to transfer real property X to D nor is assigned B's rights in B's agreement to sell real property X to D. On May 17, 1991, B transfers real property X to D and instructs D to transfer the $100,000 to C. On June 1, 1991, B identifies real property M as replacement property. On August 9, 1991, C purchases real property L from E for $100,000, and E executes and delivers to C a deed conveying real property M to C. On the same date, C executes and delivers to B a deed conveying real property M to B.

(ii) Because B transferred real property X directly to D under B's agreement with D, C did not acquire real property X from B and transfer real property X to D. Moreover, because C did not acquire legal title to real property X, did not enter into an agreement with D to transfer real property X to D, and was not assigned B's rights in B's agreement to sell real property X to D, C is not treated as acquiring and transferring real property X. Thus, C was not a qualified intermediary and paragraph (g)(4)(i) of this section does not apply.

(iii) B did not exchange real property X for real property M. Rather, B sold real property X to D and purchased, through C, real property M. Therefore, the transfer of real property X does not qualify for non recognition of gain or loss under section 1031.

(h) INTEREST AND GROWTH FACTORS —

(1) IN GENERAL. For purposes of this section, the taxpayer is treated as being entitled to receive interest or a growth factor with respect to a deferred exchange if the amount of money or property the taxpayer is entitled to receive depends upon the length of time elapsed between transfer of the relinquished property and receipt of the replacement property.

(2) TREATMENT AS INTEREST. If, as part of a deferred exchange, the taxpayer receives interest or a growth factor, the interest or growth factor will be treated as interest, regardless of whether it is paid to the taxpayer in cash or in property (including property of a like kind). The taxpayer must include the interest or growth factor in income according to the taxpayer's method of accounting.

(i) Reserved

(j) DETERMINATION OF GAIN OR LOSS RECOGNIZED AND THE BASIS OF PROPERTY RECEIVED IN A DEFERRED EXCHANGE —

(1) IN GENERAL. Except as otherwise provided, the amount of gain or loss recognized and the basis of property received in a deferred exchange is determined by applying the rules of section 1031 and the regulations there under. See sections 1.1031(b)-1, 1.1031(c)-1, 1.1031(d)-1, 1.1031(d)-1T, 1.1031(d)-2, and 1.1031(j)-1.

(2) COORDINATION WITH SECTION 453.

(i) Qualified escrow accounts and qualified trusts. Subject to the limitations of paragraphs (j)(2)(iv) and (v) of this section, in the case of a taxpayer's transfer of relinquished property in which the obligation of the taxpayer's transferee to transfer replacement property to the taxpayer is or may be secured by cash or a cash equivalent, the determination of whether the taxpayer has received a payment for purposes of section 453 and §15a.453-1(b)(3)(i) of this chapter will be made without regard to the fact that the obligation is or may be so secured if the cash or cash equivalent is held in a qualified escrow account or a qualified trust. This paragraph (j)(2)(i) ceases to apply at the earlier of—

(A) The time described in paragraph (g)(3)(iv) of this section; or

(B) The end of the exchange period.

(ii) Qualified intermediaries. Subject to the limitations of (j)(2)(iv) and (v) of this section, in the case of a taxpayer's transfer of relinquished property involving a qualified intermediary, the determination of whether the taxpayer has received a payment for purposes of section 453 and §15a.453-1(b)(3)(i) of this chapter is made as if the qualified intermediary is not the agent of the taxpayer. For purposes of this paragraph (j)(2)(ii), a person who otherwise satisfies the definition of a qualified intermediary is treated as a qualified intermediary even though that person ultimately fails to acquire identified replacement property and transfer it to the taxpayer. This paragraph (j)(2)(ii) ceases to apply at the earlier of—

(A) The time described in paragraph (g)(4)(vi) of this section; or

(B) The end of the exchange period.

(iii) Transferee indebtedness. In the case of a transaction described in paragraph (j)(2)(ii) of this section, the receipt by the taxpayer of an evidence of indebtedness of the transferee of the qualified intermediary is treated as the receipt of an evidence of indebtedness of the person acquiring property from the taxpayer for purposes of section 453 and §15a.453-1(b)(3)(i) of this chapter.

(iv) Bona fide intent requirement. The provisions of paragraphs (j)(2)(i) and (ii) of this section do not apply unless the taxpayer has a bona fide intent to enter into a deferred exchange at the beginning of the exchange period. A taxpayer will be treated as having a bona fide intent only if it is reasonable to believe, based on all the facts and circumstances as of the beginning of the exchange period, that like-kind replacement property will be acquired before the end of the exchange period.

(v) Disqualified property. The provisions of paragraphs (j)(2)(i) and (ii) of this section do not apply if the relinquished property is disqualified property. For purposes of this paragraph (j)(2), disqualified property means property that is not held for productive use in a trade or business or for investment or is property described in section 1031(a)(2).

(vi) EXAMPLES. This paragraph (j)(2) may be illustrated by the following examples. Unless otherwise provided in an example, the following facts are assumed: B is a calendar year taxpayer who agrees to enter into a deferred exchange. Pursuant to the agreement, B is to transfer real property X. Real property X, which has been held by B for investment, is unencumbered and has a fair market value of $100,000 at the time of transfer. B's adjusted basis in real property X at that time is $60,000. B identifies a single like-kind replacement property before the end of the identification period, and B receives the replacement property before the end of the exchange period. The transaction qualifies as a like-kind exchange under section 1031.

> EXAMPLE 1. (i) On September 22, 1994, B transfers real property X to C and C agrees to acquire like-kind property and deliver it to B. On that date B has a bona fide intent to enter into a deferred exchange. C's obligation, which is not payable on demand or readily tradable, is secured by $100,000 in cash. The $100,000 is deposited by C in an escrow account that is a qualified escrow account under paragraph (g)(3) of this section. The escrow agreement provides that B has no rights to receive, pledge, borrow, or otherwise obtain the benefits of the cash deposited in the escrow account until the earlier of the date the replacement property is delivered to B or the end of the exchange period. On March 11, 1995, C acquires replacement property having a fair market value of $80,000 and delivers the replacement property to B. The $20,000 in cash remaining in the qualified escrow account is distributed to B at that time.

(ii) Under section 1031(b), B recognizes gain to the extent of the $20,000 in cash that B receives in the exchange. Under paragraph (j)(2)(i) of this section, the qualified escrow account is disregarded for purposes of section 453 and §15a.453(b)(3)(i) of this chapter in determining whether B is in receipt of payment Accordingly, B's receipt of C's obligation on September 22, 1994, does not constitute a payment. Instead, B is treated as receiving payment on March 11, 1995, on receipt of the $20,000 in cash from the qualified escrow account. Subject to the other requirements of sections 453 and 453A, B may report the $20,000 gain in 1995 under the installment method. See section 453(f)(6) for special rules for determining total contract price and gross profit in the case of an exchange described in section l031(b).

> EXAMPLE 2. (i) D offers to purchase real property X but is unwilling to participate in a like-kind exchange. B thus enters into an exchange agreement with C whereby B retains C to facilitate an exchange with respect to real property X. On September 22, 1994, pursuant to the agreement, B transfers real property X to C who transfers it to D for $100,000 in cash. On that date B has a bona fide intent to enter into a deferred exchange. C is a qualified intermediary under paragraph (g)(4) of this section. The exchange agreement provides that B has no rights to receive, pledge, borrow, or otherwise obtain the benefits of the money held by C until the earlier of the date the replacement property is delivered to B or the end of the exchange period. On March 11, 1995, C acquires replacement property having a fair market value of $80,000 and delivers it, along with the remaining $20,000 from the transfer of real property X to B.

(ii) Under section 1031(b), B recognizes gain to the extent of the $20,000 cash B receives in the exchange. Under paragraph (j)(2)(ii) of this section, any agency relationship between B and C is disregarded for purposes of section 453 and §15a.453-1(b)(3)(i) of this chapter in determining whether B is in receipt of payment. Accordingly, B is not treated as having received payment on September 22, 1994, on C's receipt of payment from D for the relinquished property. Instead, B is treated as receiving payment on March 11, 1995, on receipt of the $20,000 in cash from C. Subject to the other requirements of sections 453 and 453A, B may report the $20,000 gain in 1995 under the installment method.

> EXAMPLE 3. (i) D offers to purchase real property X but is unwilling to participate in a like-kind exchange. B enters into an exchange agreement with C whereby B retains C as a qualified intermediary to facilitate an exchange with respect to real property X. On December 1, 1994, pursuant to the agreement, B transfers real property X to C who transfers it to D for $100,000 in cash. On that date B has a bona fide intent to enter into a deferred exchange. The exchange agreement provides that B has no rights to receive, pledge, borrow, or otherwise obtain the benefits of the cash held by C until the earliest of the end of the identification period if B has not identified replacement property, the date the replacement property is delivered to B, or the end of the exchange period. Although B has a bona fide intent to enter into a deferred exchange at the beginning of the exchange period, B does not identify or acquire any replacement property. In 1995, at the end of the identification period, C delivers the entire $100,000 from the sale of real property X to B.

(ii) Under Section 1001, B realizes gain to the extent of the amount realized ($100,000) over the adjusted basis in real property X ($60,000), or $40,000. Because B has a bona fide intent at the beginning of the exchange period to enter into a deferred exchange, paragraph (j)(2)(iv) of this section does not make paragraph (j)(2)(ii) of this section inapplicable even though B fails to acquire replacement property. Further, under paragraph (j)(2)(ii) of this section, C is a qualified intermediary even though C does not acquire and transfer replacement property to B. Thus, any agency relationship between B and C is disregarded for purposes of section 453 and §15a.453-1(b)(3)(i) of this chapter in determining whether B is in receipt of payment. Accordingly, B is not treated as having received payment on December 1, 1994, on C's receipt of payment from D for the relinquished property. Instead, B is treated as receiving payment at the end of the identification period in 1995 on receipt of the $100,000 in cash from C. Subject to the other requirements of sections 453 and 453A, B may report the $40,000 gain in 1995 under the installment method.

> EXAMPLE 4. (i) D offers to purchase real property X but is unwilling to participate in a like-kind exchange. B thus enters into an exchange agreement with C whereby B retains C to facilitate an exchange with respect to real property X. C is a qualified intermediary under paragraph (g)(4) of this section. On September 22, 1994, pursuant to the agreement, B transfers real property X to C who then transfers it to D for $S0,000 in cash and D's 10 year installment obligation for $20,000. On that date B has a bona fide intent to enter into a deferred exchange. The exchange agreement provides that B has no rights to receive, pledge, borrow, or otherwise obtain the benefits of the money or other property held by C until the earlier of the date the replacement property is delivered to B or the end of the exchange period. D's obligation bears adequate stated interest and is not payable on demand or readily tradable. On March 11, 1995, C acquires replacement property having a fair market value of $S0,000 and delivers it, along with the $20,000 installment obligation, to B.

(ii) Under section 1031(b), $20,000 of B's gain (i.e., the amount of the installment obligation B receives in the exchange) does not qualify for non recognition under section 1031(a). Under paragraphs (j)(2)(ii) and (iii) of this section, B's receipt of D's obligation is treated as the receipt of an obligation of the person acquiring the property for purposes of section 453 and §l5a.453-1(b)(3)(i) of this chapter in determining whether B is in receipt of payment. Accordingly, B's receipt of the obligation is not treated as a payment. Subject to the other requirements of sections 453 and 453A, B may report the $20,000 gain under the installment method on receiving payments from D on the obligation.

> EXAMPLE 5 (i) B is a corporation that has held real property X to expand its manufacturing operations. However, at a meeting in November 1994, B's directors decide that real property X is not suitable for the planned expansion, and authorize a like-kind exchange of this property for property that would be suitable for the planned expansion. B enters into an exchange agreement with C whereby B retains C as a qualified intermediary to facilitate an exchange with respect to real property X. Oh November 2S, 1994, pursuant to the agreement, B transfers real property X to C, who then transfers it to D for $100,000 in cash. The exchange agreement does not include any limitations or conditions that make it unreasonable to believe that like-kind replacement property will be acquired before the end of the exchange period. The exchange agreement provides that B has no rights to receive, pledge, borrow, or otherwise obtain the benefits of the cash held by C until the earliest of the end of the identification period, if B has not identified replacement property, the date the replacement property is delivered to B, or the end of the exchange period. In early January 1995, B's directors meet and decide that it is not feasible to proceed with the planned expansion due to a business downturn reflected in B's preliminary financial reports for the last quarter of 1994. Thus, B's directors instruct C to stop seeking replacement property C delivers the $100,000 cash to B on January 12, 1995, at the end of the identification period. Both the decision to exchange real property X for other property and the decision to cease seeking replacement property because of B's business downturn are recorded in the minutes of the directors' meetings. There are no other facts or circumstances that would indicate whether, on November 28, 1994, B had a bona fide intent to enter into a deferred like-kind exchange.

(ii) Under section 1001, B realizes gain to the extent of the amount realized ($100,000) over the adjusted basis of real property X ($60,000), or $40,000. The directors' authorization of a like-kind exchange, the terms of the exchange agreement with C, and the absence of other relevant facts, indicate that B had a bona fide intent at the beginning of the exchange period to enter into a deferred like-kind exchange. Thus, paragraph (j)(2)(iv) of this section does not make paragraph (j)(2)(ii) of this section inapplicable, even though B falls to acquire replacement property. Further, under paragraph (j)(2)(ii) of this section, C is a qualified intermediary, even though C does not transfer replacement property to B. Thus, any agency relationship between B and C is disregarded for purposes of section 453 and §15a.453-1(b)(3)(i) of this chapter in determining whether B is in receipt of payment. Accordingly, B is not treated as having received payment until January 12,1995, on receipt of the $100,000 cash from C. Subject to the other requirements of sections 453 and 453A, B may report the $40,000 gain in 1995 under the installment method.

> EXAMPLE 6. (i) B has held real property X for use in its trade or business, but decides to transfer that property because it is no longer suitable for B's planned expansion of its commercial enterprise. B and D agree to enter into a deferred exchange. Pursuant to their agreement, B transfers real property X to D on September 22, 1994, and D deposits $100,000 cash in a qualified escrow

account as security for D's obligation under the agreement to transfer replacement property to B before the end of the exchange period. D's obligation is not payable on demand or readily tradable. The agreement provides that B is not required to accept any property that is not zoned for commercial use. Before the end of the identification period, B identifies real properties J, K, and L, all zoned for residential use, as replacement properties. Any one of these properties, rezoned for commercial use, would be suitable for B's planned expansion. In recent years, the zoning board with jurisdiction over properties J, K, and L has rezoned similar properties for commercial use. The escrow agreement provides that B has no rights to receive, pledge, borrow, or otherwise obtain the benefits of the money in the escrow account until the earlier of the time that the zoning board determines, after the end of the identification period, that it will not rezone the properties for commercial use or the end of the exchange period. On January 5, 1995, the zoning board decides that none of the properties will be rezoned for commercial use. Pursuant to the exchange agreement, B receives the $100,000 cash from the escrow on January 5, 1995. There are no other facts or circumstances that would indicate whether, on September 22, 1994, B had a bona fide intent to enter into a deferred like-kind exchange.

(ii) Under section 1001, B realizes gain to the extent of the amount realized ($100,000) over the adjusted basis of real property X ($60,000), or $40,000. The terms of the exchange agreement with D, the identification of properties J, K, and L, the efforts to have those properties rezoned for commercial purposes, and the absence of other relevant facts, indicate that B had a bona fide intent at the beginning of the exchange period to enter into a deferred exchange. Moreover, the limitations imposed in the exchange agreement on acceptable replacement property do not make it unreasonable to believe that like-kind replacement property would be acquired before the end of the exchange period. Therefore, paragraph (j)(2)(iv) of this section does not make paragraph (j)(2)(i) of this section inapplicable even though B falls to acquire replacement property. Thus, for purposes of section 453 and §15a.453-1(b)(3)(i) of this chapter, the qualified escrow account is disregarded in determining whether B is in receipt of payment. Accordingly, B is not treated as having received payment on September 22, 1994, on D's deposit of the $100,000 cash into the qualified escrow account. Instead, B is treated as receiving payment on January 5,1995. Subject to the other requirements of sections 453 and 453A, B may report the $40,000 gain in 1995 under the installment method.

(vii) Effective date. This paragraph (j)(2) is effective for transfers of property occurring on or after April 20, 1994. Taxpayers may apply this paragraph (j)(2) to transfers of property occurring before April 20, 1994, but on or after June 10, 1991, if those transfers otherwise meet the requirements of §1.1031(k)-i. In addition, taxpayers may apply this paragraph (j)(2) to transfers of property occurring before June 10, 1991, but on or after May 16,1990, if those transfers otherwise meet the requirements of §l.l03l(k)-1 or follow the guidance of IA-237-S4 published in l990-1, C.B. See §60l.60l(d)(2)(ii)(b) of this chapter.

(3) EXAMPLES. This paragraph (j) may be illustrated by the following examples. Unless otherwise provided in an example, the following facts are assumed: B, a calendar year taxpayer, and C agree to enter into a deferred exchange. Pursuant to their agreement, B is to transfer real property X to C on May 17, 1991. Real property X, which has been held by B for investment, is unencumbered and has a fair market value on May 17, 1991, of $100,000. B's adjusted basis in real property X is $40,000. On or before July 1, 1991 (the end of the identification period), B is to identify replacement property that is of a like kind to real property X. On or before November 13, 1991 (the end

of the exchange period), C is required to purchase the property identified by B and to transfer that property to B. To the extent the fair market value of the replacement property transferred to B is greater or less than the fair market value of real property X, either B or C, as applicable, will make up the difference by paying cash to the other party after the date the replacement property is received. The replacement property is identified as provided in paragraph (c) of this section and is of a like kind to real property X (determined without regard to section 1031(a) (3) and this section). B intends to hold any replacement property received for investment.

EXAMPLE 1 (i) On May 17, 1991, B transfers real property X to C and identifies real property R as replacement property. On June 3, 1991, C transfers $10,000 to B. On September 4, 1991, C purchases real property R for $90,000 and transfers real property R to B.

(ii) The $10,000 received by B is "money or other property" for purposes of section 103I and the regulations there under. Under section 1031(b), B recognizes gain in the amount of $10,000. Under section 1031 (d), B' s basis in real property R is $40,000 (i.e., B's basis in real property X ($40,000), decreased in the amount of money received ($10,000), and increased in the amount of gain recognized ($10,000) in the deferred exchange).

EXAMPLE 2. (i) On May 17, 1991, B transfers real property X to C and identifies real property S as replacement property, and C transfers $10,000 to B. On September 4, 1991, C purchases real property S for $100, 000 and transfers real property 5 to B. On the same day, B transfers $10,000 to C.

(ii) The $10,000 received by B is "money or other property" for purposes of section 1031 and the regulations thereunder. Under section 1031(b), B recognizes gain in the amount of $10,000. Under section 1031(d), B's basis in real property 5 is $50,000 (i.e., B's basis in real property X ($40,000), decreased in the amount of money received ($10,000), increased in the amount of gain recognized ($10,000), and increased in the amount of the additional consideration paid by B ($10, 000) in the deferred exchange).

EXAMPLE 3 . (i) Under the exchange agreement, B has the right at all times to demand $100,000 in cash in lieu of replacement property. On May 17, 1991, B transfers real property X to C and identifies real property T as replacement property. On September 4, 1991, C purchases real property T for $100,000 and transfers real property T to B.

(ii) Because B has the right on May 17, 1991, to demand $100,000 in cash in lieu of replacement property, B is in constructive receipt of the $100,000 on that date. Thus, the transaction is a sale and not an exchange, and the $60,000 gain realized by B in the transaction (i.e., $100,000 amount realized less $40,000 adjusted basis) is recognized. Under section 1031(d), B's basis in real property T is $100, 000.

EXAMPLE 4. (i) Under the exchange agreement, B has the right at all times to demand up to $30,000 in cash and the balance in replacement property instead of receiving replacement property in the amount of $100,000. On May 17, 1991, B transfers real property X to C and identifies real property U as replacement property. On September 4, 1991, C purchases real property U for $100,000 and transfers real property U to B.

(ii) The transaction qualifies as a deferred exchange under section 1031 and this section. However, because B had the right on May 17, 1991, to demand up to $30,000 in cash, B is in constructive receipt of $30, 000 on that date. Under section 1031(b), B recognizes gain in the amount of $30,000. Under section 1031(d), B's basis in real property U is $70,000 (i.e., B's basis in real property X ($40,000), decreased in the amount of money that B received ($30, 000), increased in the amount of gain recognized ($30,000), and increased in the amount of additional consideration paid by B ($30,000) in the deferred exchange).

> EXAMPLE 5. (i) Assume real property X is encumbered by a mortgage of $30,000. On May 17, 1991, B transfers real property X to C and identifies real property V as replacement property, and C assumes the $30,000 mortgage on real property X. Real property V is encumbered by a $20,000 mortgage. On July 5, 1991, C purchases real property V for $90,000 by paying $70,000 and assuming the mortgage and transfers real property V to B with B assuming the mortgage.

(ii) The consideration received by B in the form of the liability assumed by C ($30,000) is offset by the consideration given by B in the form of the liability assumed by B ($20,000). The excess of the liability assumed by C over the liability assumed by B, $10,000, is treated as "money or other property." See section 1.1031(b)-1(c). Thus, B recognizes gain under section 1031(b) in the amount of $10,000. Under section 1031(d), B's basis in real property V is $40,000 (i.e., B's basis in real property X ($40,000), decreased in the amount of money that B is treated as receiving in the form of the liability assumed by C ($30,000), increased in the amount of money that B is treated as paying in the form of the liability assumed by B ($20,000), and increased in the amount of the gain recognized ($10,000) in the deferred exchange).

(k) DEFINITION OF DISQUALIFIED PERSON.

(1) For purposes of this section, a disqualified person is a person described in paragraph (k)(2), (k)(3), or (k)(4) of this section.

(2) The person is the agent of the taxpayer at the time of the transaction. For this purpose, a person who has acted as the taxpayer's employee, attorney, accountant, investment banker or broker, or real estate agent or broker within the 2-year period ending on the date of the transfer of the first of the relinquished properties is treated as an agent of the taxpayer at the time of the transaction. Solely for purposes of this paragraph (k)(2), performance of the following services will not be taken into account—

> (i) Services for the taxpayer with respect to exchanges of property intended to qualify for non recognition of gain or loss under section 1031; and

> (ii) Routine financial, title insurance, escrow, or trust services for the taxpayer by a financial institution, title insurance company, or escrow company.

(3) The person and the taxpayer bear a relationship described in either section 267(b) or section 707(b) (determined by substituting in each section "10 percent" for "50 percent" each place it appears).

(4) (i) Except as provided in paragraph (k)(4)(ii) of this section, the person and a person described in paragraph (k)(2) of this section bear a relationship described in either section 267(b) or section 707(b) (determined by substituting in each section "10 percent" for "50 percent" each place it appears).

> (ii) In the case of a transfer of relinquished property made by a taxpayer on or after January 17, 2001, paragraph (k)(4)(i) of this section does not apply to a bank (as defined in section 581) or a bank af-

filiate if, but for this paragraph (k)(4)(ii), the bank or bank affiliate would be a disqualified person under paragraph (k)(4)(i) of this section solely because it is a member of the same controlled group (as determined under section 267(f)(1), substituting "10 percent" for "50 percent" where it appears) as a person that has provided investment banking or brokerage services to the taxpayer within the 2-year period described in paragraph (k)(2) of this section. For purposes of this paragraph (k)(4)(ii), a bank affiliate is a corporation whose principal activity is rendering services to facilitate exchanges of property intended to qualify for nonrecognition of gain under section 1031 and all of whose stock is owned by either the bank or a bank holding company (within the meaning of section2(a) of the Bank Holding Company Act of 1956 (12 U.S.C. 1841 (a)).

(5) This paragraph (k) may be illustrated by the following examples. Unless otherwise provided, the following facts are assumed: On May 1, 1991, B enters into an exchange agreement (as defined in paragraph (g)(4)(iii)(B) of this section) with C whereby B retains C to facilitate an exchange with respect to real property X. On May 17, 1991, pursuant to the agreement, B executes and delivers to C a deed conveying real property X to C. C has no relationship to B described in paragraphs (k)(2), (k)(3), or (k)(4) of this section.

>EXAMPLE 1. (i) C is B's accountant and has rendered accounting services to B within the 2-year period ending on May 17, 1991, other than with respect to exchanges of property intended to qualify for non recognition of gain or loss under section 1031.

(ii) C is a disqualified person because C has acted as B's accountant within the 2-year period ending on May 17, 1991.

(iii) If C had not acted as B's accountant within the 2-year period ending on May 17, 1991, or if C had acted-as B's accountant within that period only with respect to exchanges intended to qualify-for non recognition of gain or loss under section 1031, C would not have been a disqualified person.

>EXAMPLE 2. (i) C, which is engaged in the trade or business of acting as an intermediary to facilitate deferred exchanges, is a wholly owned subsidiary of an escrow company that has performed routine escrow services for B in the past. C has previously been retained by B to act as an intermediary in prior section 1031 exchanges.

(ii) C is not a disqualified person notwithstanding the intermediary services previously provided by C to B (see paragraph (k)(2)(i) of this section) and notwithstanding the combination of C's relationship to the escrow company and the escrow services previously provided by the escrow company to B (see paragraph (k)(2)(ii) of this section).

>EXAMPLE 3. (i) C is a corporation that is only engaged in the trade or business of acting as an intermediary to facilitate deferred exchanges. Each of 10 law firms owns 10 percent of the outstanding stock of C. One of the 10 law firms that owns 10 percent of C is M. J is the managing partner of M and is the president of C. J, in his capacity as a partner in M, has also rendered legal advice to B within the 2-year period ending on May 17, 1991, on matters other than exchanges intended to qualify for non recognition of gain or loss under section 1031.

(ii) J and M are disqualified persons. C, however, is not a disqualified person because neither J nor M own, directly or indirectly, more than 10 percent of the stock of C. Similarly, J's participation in the management of C does not make C a disqualified person.

(l) Reserved

(m) DEFINITION OF FAIR MARKET VALUE. For purposes of this section, the fair market value of property means the fair market value of the property without regard to any liabilities secured by the property.

(n) NO INFERENCE WITH RESPECT TO ACTUAL OR CONSTRUCTIVE RECEIPT RULES OUTSIDE OF SECTION 1031. The rules provided in this section relating to actual or constructive receipt are intended to be rules for determining whether there is actual or constructive receipt in the case of a deferred exchange. No inference is intended regarding the application of these rules for purposes of determining whether actual or constructive receipt exists for any other purpose.

(o) EFFECTIVE DATE. This section applies to transfers of property made by a taxpayer on or after June 10, 1991. However, a transfer of property made by a taxpayer on or after May 16, 1990, but before June 10, 1991 will be treated as complying with section 1031(a)(3) and this section if the deferred exchange satisfies either the provisions of this section or the provisions of the notice of proposed rule-making published in the Federal Register on May 16, 1990 (55 F.R. 20278).

Notes

IRC § 1031.
EXCHANGE OF PROPERTY HELD FOR PRODUCTIVE USE OR INVESTMENT.

(a)   **Nonrecognition of Gain or Loss From Exchanges Solely in Kind.--**

(1)   **In general.--**No gain or loss shall be recognized on the exchange of property held for productive use in a trade or business or for investment if such property is exchanged solely for property of like kind which is to be held either for productive use in a trade or business or for investment.

(2)   **Exception.--**This subsection shall not apply to any exchange of--
(A)   stock in trade or other property held primarily for sale,
(B)   stocks, bonds, or notes,
(C)   other securities or evidences of indebtedness or interest,
(D)   interests in a partnership,
(E)   certificates of trust or beneficial interests, or
(F)   choses in action.

For purposes of this section, an interest in a partnership which has, in effect, a valid election under section 761(a) to be excluded from the application of all of subchapter K shall be treated as an interest in each of the assets of such partnership and not as an interest in a partnership.

(3)   **Requirement that property be identified and that exchange be completed not more than 180 days after transfer of exchanged property.--**For purposes of this subsection, any property received by the taxpayer shall be treated as property which is not like-kind property if--

(A)   such property is not identified as property to be received in the exchange on or before the day, which is 45 days after the date on which the taxpayer transfers the property relinquished in the exchange, or

(B)   such property is received after the earlier of--

(i)   the day which is 180 days after the date on which the taxpayer transfers the property relinquished in the exchange, or
(ii)   the due date (determined with regard to extension) for the transferor's return of the tax imposed by this chapter for the taxable year in which the transfer of the relinquished property occurs.

(b)   **Gain From Exchanges Not Solely in Kind.--**If an exchange would be within the provisions of subsection (a), of section 1035(a), of section 1036(a), or of section 1037(a), if it were not for the fact that the property received in exchange consists not only of property permitted by such provisions to be received without the recognition of gain, but also of other property or money, then the gain, if any, to the recipient shall be recognized, but in an amount not in excess of the sum of such money and the fair market value of such other property.

(c)   **Loss From Exchanges Not Solely in Kind.**--If an exchange would be within the provisions of subsection (a), of section 1035(a), or section 1036(a), or of section 1037(a), if it were not for the fact that the property received in exchange consists not only of property permitted by such provisions to be received without the recognition of gain or loss, but also of other property or money, then no loss from the exchange shall be recognized.

(d)   **Basis.**--If property was acquired on an exchange described in this section, section 1035(a), section 1036(a), or of section 1037(a), then the basis shall be the same as that of the property exchanged, decreased in the amount of any money received by the taxpayer and increased in the amount of gain or decreased in the amount of loss to the taxpayer that was recognized on such exchange. If the property so acquired consisted in part of the type of property permitted by this section, section 1035(a), section 1036(a), or of section 1037(a), to be received without the recognition of gain or loss, and in part of other property, the basis provided in this subsection shall be allocated between the properties (other than money) received, and for the purpose of the allocation there shall be assigned to such other property an amount equivalent to its fair market value at the date of the exchange. For purposes of this section, section 1035(a), and section 1036(a), where as part of the consideration to the taxpayer another party to the exchange assumed a liability of the taxpayer or acquired from the taxpayer property subject to a liability, such assumption or acquisition (in the amount of the liability) shall be considered as money received by the taxpayer on the exchange.

(e)   **Exchanges of Livestock of Different Sexes.**--For purposes of this section, livestock of different sexes are not property of a like kind.

(f)   **Special Rules for Exchanges Between Related Persons.**--

(1)   **In general.**--If--

(A)   a taxpayer exchanges property with a related person.
(B)   there is non-recognition of gain or loss to the taxpayer under this section with respect to the exchange of such property (determined without regard to this subsection), and
(C)   before the date 2 years after the date of the last transfer which was part of such exchange--

(i)   the related person disposes of such property, or
(ii)   the taxpayer disposes of the property received in the exchange from the related person which was of like kind to the property transferred by the taxpayer, there shall be no non-recognition of gain or loss under this section to the taxpayer with respect to such exchange; except that any gain or loss recognized by the taxpayer by reason of this subsection shall be taken into account as of the date on which the disposition referred to in subparagraph (C) occurs.

(2)   **Certain dispositions not taken into account.**--For purposes of paragraph (1)(C), there shall not be taken into account any disposition--

(A)   after the earlier of the death of the taxpayer or the death of the related person,

(B)   in a compulsory or involuntary conversion (within the meaning of section 1033) if the exchange occurred before the threat or imminence of such conversion, or

(C)   with respect to which it is established to the satisfaction of the Secretary that neither the exchange nor such disposition had as one of its principal purposes the avoidance of Federal income tax.

(3)   **Related person.**--For purposes of this subsection, the term "related person" means any person bearing a relationship to the taxpayer described in §267(B) or § 707(b)(1).

(4)   **Treatment of certain transactions.**--This section shall not apply to any exchange which is part of a transaction (or series of transactions) structured to avoid the purposes of this subsection.

(g)   **Special Rule Where Substantial Diminution of Risk.**--

(1)   **In general.**--If paragraph (2) applies to any property for any period, the running of the period set forth in subsection (f)(1)(C) with respect to such property shall be suspended during such period.

(2)   **Property to which subsection applies.**--This paragraph shall apply to any property for any period during which the holder's risk of loss with respect to the property is substantially diminished by--

(A)   the holding of a put with respect to such property,

(B)   the holding by another person of a right to acquire such property, or

(C)   a short sale or any other transaction.

(h)   **Special Rules for Foreign Real and Personal Property.**-- For purposes of this section--

(1)   **Real Property.**-- Real property located in the United States and real property located outside the United States are not property of a like kind.

(2)   **Personal Property.**--

(A)   **In General.**-- Personal property used predominantly within the United States and personal property used predominantly outside the United States are not property of a like kind.

(B)   **Predominant Use.**-- Except as provided in subparagraph (C) and (D), the predominant use of any property shall be determined based on--

(i)   in the case of the property relinquished in the exchange, the 2-year period ending on the date of such relinquishment, and

(ii)   in the case of the property acquired in the exchange, the 2-year period beginning on the date of such acquisition.

(C)   **Property held for less than 2 years.**-- Except in the case of an exchange which is part of a transaction (or series of transactions) structured to avoid the purposes of this subsection--

(i)   only the periods the property was held by the person relinquishing the property (or any related person) shall be taken into account under subparagraph (B)(i), and

(ii)   only the periods the property was held by the person acquiring the property (or any related person) shall be taken into account under subparagraph (B)(ii).

(D)   **Special Rule for Certain Property.**-- Property described in any subparagraph of section 168(g)(4) shall be treated as used predominantly in the United States.

Appendix C

Appendix C

INTERNAL REVENUE PROCEDURE 2000-37 (REVERSE EXCHANGES)

SECTION 1. PURPOSE

This revenue procedure provides a safe harbor under which the Internal Revenue Service will not challenge (a) the qualification of property as either "replacement property" or "relinquished property" (as defined in § 1.1031(k)-1(a) of the Income Tax Regulations) for purposes of § 1031 of the Internal Revenue Code and the regulations thereunder or (b) the treatment of the "exchange accommodation titleholder" as the beneficial owner of such property for federal income tax purposes, if the property is held in a "qualified exchange accommodation arrangement" (QEAA), as defined in section 4.02 of this revenue procedure.

SECTION 2. BACKGROUND

.01 Section 1031(a)(1) provides that no gain or loss is recognized on the exchange of property held for productive use in a trade or business or for investment if the property is exchanged solely for property of like kind that is to be held either for productive use in a trade or business or for investment.

.02 Section 1031(a)(3) provides that property received by the taxpayer is not treated as like-kind property *if* it: (a) is not identified as property to be received in the exchange on or before the day that is 45 days after the date on which the taxpayer transfers the relinquished property; or (b) is received after the earlier of the date that is 180 days after the date on which the taxpayer transfers the relinquished property, or the due date (determined with regard to extension) for the transferor's federal income tax return for the year in which the transfer of the relinquished property occurs.

.03 Determining the owner of property for federal income tax purposes requires an analysis of all of the facts and circumstances. As a general rule, the party that bears the economic burdens and benefits of ownership will be considered the owner of property for federal income tax purposes. See Rev. Rul. 82-144, 1982-2 C.B. 34.

.04 On April 25, 1991, the Treasury Department and the Service promulgated final regulations under § 1.1031(k)-1 providing rules for deferred like-kind exchanges under § 1031(a)(3). The preamble to the final regulations states that the deferred exchange rules under § 1031(a)(3) do not apply to reverse-Starker exchanges (i.e., exchange where the replacement property is acquired before the relinquished property is transferred) and consequently that the final regulations do not apply to such exchanges. T.D. 8346, 1991-1 C.B. 150, 15k see Starker v. United States, 602 F.2d 1341 (91h Cir. 1979). However, the preamble indicates that Treasury and the Service will continue to study the applicability of the general rule of § 1031(a)(1) to these transactions. T.D. 8346, 1991-1 C.B. 150, 151.

.05 Since the promulgation of the final regulations under § 1.1031(k)-1, taxpayers have engaged in a wide variety of transactions, including so-called "parking" transactions, to facilitate reverse like-kind exchanges. Parking transactions typically are designed to "park" the desired replacement property with an accommodation party until such time as the taxpayer arranges for the transfer of the relinquished property to the ultimate transferee in a simultaneous or deferred exchange. Once such a transfer is arranged, the taxpayer transfers the relinquished property to the accommodation party in exchange for the replacement property, and the accommodation party then transfers the relinquished property to the ultimate transferee. In other situations, an accommodation party may acquire the desired replacement property on behalf of the taxpayer and immediately change such property with the taxpayer for the relinquished property, thereafter holding the relinquished property until the taxpayer arranges for a transfer of such property to the ultimate transferee. In the parking arrangements, taxpayers attempt to arrange the transaction so that the accommodation party has enough of the benefits and burdens relating to the property so that the accommodation party will be treated as the owner for federal income tax purposes.

.06 Treasury and the Service have determined that it is in the best interest of sound tax administration to provide taxpayers with a workable means of qualifying their transactions under § 1031 in situations where the taxpayer has a genuine intent to accomplish a like-kind exchange at the time that it arranges for the acquisition of the replacement property and actually accomplishes the exchange within a short time thereafter. Accordingly, this revenue procedure provides a safe harbor that allows a taxpayer to treat the accommodation party as the owner of the property for federal income tax purposes, thereby enabling the taxpayer to accomplish a qualifying like-kind exchange.

SECTION 3. SCOPE

.01 Exclusivity. This revenue procedure provides a safe harbor for the qualification under § 1031 of certain arrangements between taxpayers and exchange accommodation titleholders and provides for the treatment of the exchange accommodation titleholder as the beneficial owner of the property for federal income tax purposes. These provisions apply only in the limited context described in this revenue procedure. The principles set forth in this revenue procedure have no application to any federal income tax determinations other than determinations that involve arrangements qualifying for the safe harbor.

.02 No inference. No inference is intended with respect to the federal income tax treatment of arrangements similar to those described in this revenue procedure that were entered into prior to the effective date of this revenue procedure. Further, the Service recognizes that "parking" transactions can be accomplished outside of the safe harbor provided in this revenue procedure. Accordingly, no inference is intended with respect to the federal income tax treatment of "parking" transactions that do not satisfy the terms of the safe harbor provided in this revenue procedure, whether entered into prior to or after the effective date of this revenue procedure.

.03 Other issues. Services for the taxpayer in connection with a person's role as the exchange accommodation titleholder in a QEAA shall not be taken into account in determining whether that person or a related person is a disqualified person (as defined in § 1.1031(k)-1(k)). Even though property will not fail to be treated as being held in a QEAA as a result of one or more arrangements described in section 4.03 of this revenue procedure, the Service still may recast an amount paid pursuant to such an arrangement as a fee paid to the exchange accommodation titleholder for acting as an exchange accommodation titleholder to the extent necessary to reflect the true economic substance of the arrangement. Other federal income tax issues implicated, but not addressed, in this revenue procedure include the treatment, for federal income tax purposes, of payments described in section 4.03(7) and whether an exchange accommodation titleholder may be precluded from claiming depreciation deductions as a dealer with respect to the relinquished property or the replacement property.

.04 <u>Effect of Noncompliance</u>. If the requirements of this revenue procedure are not satisfied (for example, the property subject to a QEAA is not transferred within the time period provided), then this revenue procedure does not apply. Accordingly, the determination of whether the taxpayer or the exchange accommodation titleholder is the owner of the property for federal income tax purposes, and the proper treatment of any transactions entered into by or between parties, will be made without regard to the provisions of this revenue procedure.

SECTION 4. QUALIFIED EXCHANGE ACCOMMODATION ARRANGEMENTS

.01 <u>Generally</u>. The Service will not challenge the qualification of property as either "replacement property" or "relinquished property" (as defined in § 1.1031(k)-1(a)) for purposes of § 1031 and the regulations thereunder, or the treatment of the exchange accommodation titleholder as the beneficial owner of such property for federal income tax purposes, if the property is held in a QEAA.

.02 <u>Qualified Exchange Accommodation Arrangements</u>. For purposes of this revenue procedure, property is held in a QEAA if all of the following requirements are met:

(1) Qualified indicia of ownership of the property is held by a person (the "exchange accommodation titleholder") who is not the taxpayer or a disqualified person and either such person is subject to federal income tax or, if such person is treated as a partnership or S corporation for federal income tax purposes, more than 90 percent of its interest or stock are owned by partners or shareholders who are subject to federal income tax. Such qualified indicia of ownership must be held by the exchange accommodation titleholder at all times from the date of acquisition by the exchange accommodation titleholder until the property is transferred as described in section 4.02(5) of this revenue procedure. For this purpose, "qualified indicia of ownership" means legal title to the property, other indicia of ownership of the property that are treated as beneficial ownership of the property under applicable principles of commercial law (e.g., a contract for deed), or interests in an entity that is disregarded as an entity separate from its owner for federal income tax purposes (e.g., a single member limited liability company) and that holds either legal title to the property or such other indicia of ownership.;

(2) At the time the qualified indicia of ownership of the property is transferred to the exchange accommodation titleholder, it is the taxpayer's bona fide intent that the property held by the exchange accommodation titleholder represent either replacement property or relinquished property in an exchange that is intended to qualify for nonrecognition of gain (in whole or in part) or loss under § 1031;

(3) No later than five business days after the transfer of qualified indicia of ownership of the property to the exchange accommodation titleholder, the taxpayer and the exchange accommodation titleholder enter into a written agreement (the "qualified exchange accommodation agreement") that provides that the exchange accommodation titleholder is holding the property for the benefit of the taxpayer in order to facilitate an exchange under § 1031 and this revenue procedure and that the taxpayer and the exchange accommodation titleholder agree to report the acquisition, holding, and disposition of the property as provided in this revenue procedure. The agreement must specify that the exchange accommodation titleholder will be treated as the beneficial owner of the property for all federal income tax purposes. Both parties must report the federal income tax attributes of the property on their federal income tax returns in a manner consistent with this agreement.

(4) No later than 45 days after the transfer of qualified indicia of ownership of the replacement property 'he exchange accommodation titleholder, the relinquished property is properly identified. Identification must be made in a manner consistent with the principles described in § 1.1031(k)-1(c). For purposes of this section, the taxpayer may properly identify alternative and multiple properties, as described in § 1.1031(k)-1(c)(4);

(5) No later than 180 days after the transfer of qualified indicia of ownership of the property to the exchange accommodation titleholder, (a) the property is transferred (either directly or indirectly through a qualified intermediary (as defined in § 1.1031(k)-1(g)(4)) to the taxpayer as replacement property; or (b) the property is transferred to a person who is not the taxpayer or a disqualified person as relinquished property; and

(6) The combined time period that the relinquished property and the replacement property are held in a QEAA does not exceed 180 days.

.03 Permissible Agreements. Property will not fail to be treated as being held in a QEAA as a result of any one or more of the following legal or contractual arrangements, regardless of whether such arrangements contain terms that typically would result from arm's length bargaining between unrelated parties with respect to such arrangements:

(1) An exchange accommodation titleholder that satisfied the requirements of the qualified intermediary safe harbor set for in § 1.1031(k)-1(g)(4) may enter into an exchange agreement with the taxpayer to serve as the qualified intermediary in a simultaneous or deferred exchange of the property under § 1031;

(2) The taxpayer or a disqualified person guarantees some or all of the obligations of the exchange accommodation titleholder, including secured or unsecured debt incurred to acquire the property, or indemnifies the exchange accommodation titleholder against costs an expenses;

(3) The taxpayer or a disqualified person loans or advances funds to the exchange accommodation titleholder or guarantees a loan or advance to the exchange accommodation titleholder;

(4) The property is leased by the exchange accommodation titleholder to the taxpayer or a disqualified person;

(5) The taxpayer or a disqualified person manages the property, supervises improvement of the property, acts as a contractor, or otherwise provides services to the exchange accommodation titleholder with respect to the property;

(6) The taxpayer and the exchange accommodation titleholder enter into agreements or arrangements relating to the purchase or sale of the property, including puts and calls at fixed or formula prices, effective for a period not in excess of 185 days from the date the property is acquired by the exchange accommodation titleholder; and

(7) The taxpayer and the exchange accommodation titleholder enter into agreements or arrangements providing that any variation in the value of a relinquished property from the estimated value on the date of the

exchange accommodation titleholder's receipt of the property be taken into account upon the exchange accommodation titleholder's disposition of the relinquished property through the taxpayer's advance of funds to, or receipt of funds from, the exchange accommodation titleholder.

.04 Permissible Treatment. Property will not fail to be treated as being held in a QEAA merely because the accounting, regulatory, or state, local, or foreign tax treatment of the arrangement between the taxpayer and the exchange accommodation titleholder is different from the treatment required by section 4.02(3) of this revenue procedure.

SECTION 5. EFFECTIVE DATE

The revenue procedure is effective for QEAAs entered into with respect to an exchange accommodation titleholder that acquires qualified indicia of ownership of property on or after September 15, 2000.

SECTION 6. PAPERWORK REDUCTION ACT

The collections of information contained in this revenue procedure have been reviewed and approved by the Office of Management and Budget in accordance with the Paperwork Reduction Act (44 U.S.C. 3507) under control number 1545-1701. An agency may not conduct or sponsor, and a person is not required to respond to, a collection of information unless the collection of information displays a valid control number.

The collections of information are contained in section 4.02 of this revenue procedure, which requires taxpayers and exchange accommodation titleholders to enter into a written agreement that the exchange accommodation titleholder will be treated as the beneficial owner of the property for all federal income tax purposes. This information is required to ensure that both parties to a QEAA treat the transaction consistently for federal tax purposes. The likely respondents are businesses and other for-profit institutions, and individuals.

The estimated average annual burden to prepare the agreement and certification is two hours. The estimated number of respondents is 1,600, and the estimated total annual reporting burden is 3,200 hours.

The estimated annual frequency of responses is on occasion.

Books and records relating to a collection of information must be retained as long as their contents may become material in the administration of any internal revenue law. Generally, tax returns and tax return information are confidential, as required by 26 U.S.C. 6103.

DRAFTING INFORMATION

The principal author of this revenue procedure is J. Peter Baumgarten of the Office of Associate Chief Counsel (Income Tax and Accounting). For further information regarding this revenue procedure, contact Mr. Baumgarten on (202) 622-4950 (not a toll-free call).

IRS NOTICE 2005-3 (I.R.B. 2005-5, JANUARY 31, 2005)

Extension of Exchange Time Limits in a Presidentially Declared Disaster

This notice advises taxpayers that the Internal Revenue Service and Treasury Department will modify retroactively Rev. Proc. 2004-13, 2004-4 I.R.B. 335, to provide additional tax relief to taxpayers (transferors) involved in § 1031 like-kind exchange transactions affected by a Presidentially declared disaster, a terroristic or military action, service in a combat zone, or service with respect to contingency operations. Rev. Proc. 2004-13 will be modified to expand the list of time-sensitive acts under §§ 7508 and 7508A as described below under EXPANDED LIST OF TIME-SENSITIVE ACTS. Rev. Proc. 2004-13 also will be modified as described below under SPECIAL RELIEF FOR § 1031 TRANSACTIONS to (1) expand the categories of taxpayers qualifying for relief, and (2) provide additional postponements of certain § 1031 deadlines.

Under this notice, taxpayers are entitled immediately to additional tax relief if, with respect to a Presidentially declared disaster, the Service has issued an IRS News Release or other guidance authorizing postponement of deadlines under § 7508A. For example, additional relief under this notice is immediately available to victims of Hurricanes Charley, Frances, Ivan and Jeanne, and Tropical Storm Bonnie, who were granted relief in prior IRS News Releases. Taxpayers may rely on this notice until Rev. Proc. 2004-13 is modified as described in this notice.

BACKGROUND

Under § 1031, taxpayers generally do not recognize gain or loss on the exchange of property held for productive use in a trade or business or for investment if such property is exchanged solely for property of like kind that is to be held either for productive use in a trade or business or for investment. In the case of a deferred like-kind exchange under § 1031(a)(3), however, two particular requirements must be met. First, replacement property must be identified by midnight of the 45th day after the taxpayer transfers the relinquished property (45-day identification period). Section 1.1031(k)-1(b)(2)(i) of the Income Tax Regulations. Second, under § 1.1031(k)-1(b)(2)(ii), the taxpayer must receive the replacement property by midnight of the earlier of—

(1) The 180th day after the taxpayer transfers the relinquished property (180-day exchange period); or

(2) The due date (including extensions) of the taxpayer's income tax return for the taxable year in which the taxpayer transferred the relinquished property (due date of return exchange period).

Rev. Proc. 2000-37, 2000-2 C.B. 308, modified by Rev. Proc. 2004-51, 2004-33 I.R.B. 294, provides a safe harbor under which transactions will qualify for treatment under § 1031 if a taxpayer meets the requirements of a 5-business day period to enter into a qualified exchange accommodation agreement (QEAA), a 45-day identification period, a 180-day exchange period, and a 180-day combined time period, which are set forth in section 4.02(3) through (6) of Rev. Proc. 2000-37.

Generally, section 7508 postpones the time for performing specified acts for individuals serving in the Armed Forces of the United States, or serving in support of such Armed Forces, in a combat zone, or with respect to a contingency operation.

Generally, section 7508A permits the Secretary to postpone specified deadlines for taxpayers affected by a Presidentially declared disaster (as defined in § 1033(h)(3)) or a terroristic or military action (as defined in § 692(c)(2)).

Rev. Proc. 2004-13 provides an updated list of time sensitive acts, the performance of which may be postponed under §§ 7508 and 7508A. The list of acts in Rev. Proc. 2004-13 supplements the list of acts that are *automatically* postponed under § 7508 and the list of acts in the regulations under § 7508A for which the Service may authorize postponements. Rev. Proc. 2004-13 does not itself entitle taxpayers to any postponements under § 7508 or § 7508A. Rather, for taxpayers to be entitled to a postponement with respect to any act listed in Rev. Proc. 2004-13, the Service generally will issue an IRS News Release or other guidance providing such relief with respect to a specific Presidentially declared disaster area, terroristic or military action, service in a combat zone, or service with respect to contingency operations.

EXPANDED LIST OF TIME-SENSITIVE ACTS

Section 6 of Rev. Proc. 2004-13 will be modified to add to the list of time-sensitive acts, the performance of which may be postponed under §§ 7508 and 7508A, the acts described in section 4.02(3), (4), (5) and (6) of Rev. Proc. 2000-37, modified by Rev. Proc. 2004-51, relating to certain like-kind exchanges of property under § 1031.

SPECIAL RELIEF FOR § 1031 TRANSACTIONS

Overview

Rev. Proc. 2004-13 also will be modified to include a 120-day postponement for meeting certain § 1031 like-kind exchange deadlines under the circumstances set forth below under *General Rule* and *Additional Relief for Substantially Damaged Identified Property*. Taxpayers may use the postponement rules provided by this notice in lieu of the general extension dates provided by the IRS News Release or other guidance issued with respect to a specific Presidentially declared disaster. The deadlines to which the 120-day postponements apply are—

(1) The 45-day identification period and the 180-day exchange period (*but not the due date of return exchange period*) for deferred like-kind exchanges set forth in § 1.1031(k)-1(b)(2); and

(2) The 5-business day period to enter into a QEAA, the 45-day identification period, the 180-day exchange period, and the 180-day combined time period set forth in section 4.02(3) through (6) of Rev. Proc. 2000-37, modified by Rev. Proc. 2004-51.

General Rule

The last day of a 45-day identification period set forth in § 1.1031(k)-1(b)(2), the last day of a 180-day exchange period set forth in § 1.1031(k)-1(b)(2), and the last day of a period set forth in section 4.02(3) through (6) of Rev. Proc. 2000-37, modified by Rev. Proc. 2004-51, that falls on or after the date of a Presidentially declared disaster is postponed by 120 days or to the last day of the general disaster extension period authorized by an IRS News Release or other guidance announcing tax relief for victims of the specific Presidentially declared disaster, whichever is later.

A taxpayer who is a transferor qualifies for a postponement under the *General Rule* only if—

(1) The relinquished property was transferred on or before the date of the Presidentially declared disaster, or in a transaction governed by Rev. Proc. 2000-37, modified by Rev. Proc. 2004-51, qualified *indicia* of ownership were transferred to the exchange accommodation titleholder on or before that date; and

(2) The taxpayer (transferor)—

(a) Is an "affected taxpayer" as defined in § 301.7508A-1(d)(1) of the Procedure and Administration Regulations; or

(b) Has difficulty meeting the 45-day identification or 180-day exchange deadline set forth in § 1.1031(k)-1(b)(2), or a deadline set forth in section 4.02(3) through (6) of Rev. Proc. 2000-37, modified by Rev. Proc. 2004-51, due to the Presidentially declared disaster for the following or similar reasons:

(i) The relinquished property or the replacement property is located in a covered disaster area (as defined in § 301.7508A-1(d)(2)) as provided in the IRS News Release or other guidance (the covered disaster area);

(ii) The principal place of business of any party to the transaction (for example, a qualified intermediary, exchange accommodation titleholder, transferee, settlement attorney, lender, financial institution, or a title insurance company) is located in the covered disaster area;

(iii) Any party to the transaction (or an employee of such a party who is involved in the § 1031 transaction) is killed, injured, or missing as a result of the Presidentially declared disaster;

(iv) A document prepared in connection with the exchange (for example, the agreement between the transferor and the qualified intermediary or the deed to the relinquished property or replacement property) or a relevant land record is destroyed, damaged, or lost as a result of the Presidentially declared disaster;

(v) A lender decides not to fund either permanently or temporarily a real estate closing due to the Presidentially declared disaster or refuses to fund a loan to the taxpayer because flood, disaster, or other hazard insurance is not available due to the Presidentially declared disaster; or

(vi) A title insurance company is not able to provide the required title insurance policy necessary to settle or close a real estate transaction due to the Presidentially declared disaster.

Additional Relief for Substantially Damaged Identified Property

The postponement described in the *General Rule* also applies to the last day of a 45-day identification period described in § 1.1031(k)-1(b)(2) and the last day of a 45-day identification period described in section 4.05(4) of Rev. Proc. 2000-37, modified by Rev. Proc. 2004-51, that falls prior to the date of a Presidentially declared disaster if an identified replacement property (in the case of an exchange described in § 1.1031(k)-1), or an identified relinquished property (in the case of an exchange described in Rev. Proc. 2000-37, modified by Rev. Proc. 2004-51) is substantially damaged by the Presidentially declared disaster.

EFFECTIVE DATE

Taxpayers may apply the proposed modifications to Rev. Proc. 2004-13 described in this notice for acts that may be performed on or after January 26, 2004, the effective date of Rev. Proc. 2004-13.

DRAFTING INFORMATION

The principal author of this notice is Michael F. Schmit of the Office of Associate Chief Counsel (Income Tax and Accounting). For further information regarding this notice, contact Mr. Schmit at (202) 622-4960 or J. Peter Baumgarten at (202) 622-4920 (not toll-free calls).

INDEX